Old Librarians Never Die
They Jump out of Airplanes

Adventuring Through the Senior Years in Indiana

Marie J. Albertson

Hawthorne Publishing
15601 Oak Road
Carmel
IN 46033

© 2012 Marie J. Albertson

All rights reserved. No part of this publication may be reproduced or transmitted in any form or by any means electronic or mechanical, including photocopy, recording, or any information storage and retrival system, without permission in writing from the copyright holder.

Cover design: Wilson Design, LLC
All photos are from the author's collection

ISBN: 978-0-9831994-4-1

Dedication

To all the strong women I have had the pleasure of knowing in my past and present, including my daughters Colette and Tamara and daughter-in-law Windy.

Also for my dear friend Helen, who encouraged me to develop the discipline to write every day.

This does not mean I don't appreciate strong men too: my sons Bob and Chuck are great examples.

Table of Contents

1 Introduction 1

Section I: Envisioning Adventure **5**

2 Being Adventuresome is Cultivated, but You're Also Born That Way Sometimes. 6

3 Living in Two Worlds: A New Phase Is Coming................. 13

4 What's a Nice, Mild-mannered Librarian Like Me Doing in a Mess Like This?. 22

Section II: Adventuring Through Travel **31**

5 Destination: China. 32

6 Destination: Alaska. 37

7 Destination: The Galapagos Islands 42

8 Destination: Morocco.. 46

9 Destination: Australia.. 50

10 Destination: Europe: Ireland, Paris, Spain........................ 54

11 Destination: Egypt 59

Section III: Adventuring Beyond the Boundaries **68**

12 Learning To Kayak.. 69

13 Stranded at the Train Station 74

14 Running for Public Office 77

15 Skiing 80

16 Picture on a Nude Beach 83

17 Mustangs... 85

18 Parachuting—Jumping for Joy 90

19 Trapezing... 94

20 Trying the Triathlon 97

21 Tall Ships 101

22 Gliding 104

23 Pole Dancing 106

Section IV: Adventures of the Mind and Spirit 111

24 Present Tense Only, Please 112

25 Shyness 117

26 Putting Your Own Stamp on Religious Experience: or Not. 119

27 The Facelift 122

28 Getting a Little Culture On: Shakespeare 125

29 Talking to Spiders 128

30 Electronic Adventuring—The Last Frontier 131

31 The Hypnotist: Off the Beaten Path for Sure 134

32 The Ultimate Adventure—Writing a Book 137

What are you waiting for? How will you know pole dancing isn't for you if you don't learn about it and maybe—get dancing. Or doing any of the other, probably more approachable, activities I suggest for your senior adventuring.

1
Introduction

Librarians are no longer known as little old ladies with hair buns, at least not this keeper of books. Forget that! Since retiring at the age of seventy, I have traveled alone around the world. I have visited every continent except Antarctica. In these travels I have walked the Great Wall of China, frolicked with sea lions in the Galapagos Islands, snorkeled on the Great Barrier Reef in Australia, and ridden a camel in the Sahara. I have experienced a balloon ride over Marrakesh, kayaked on the Coral Sea, and encountered a medicine man in the Amazon jungle. At age sixty-five I took kayaking lessons and kayaked most of the rivers of western America. And yes, I have parachuted out of an airplane. Along the way I have gained perspectives for living. For example, through kayaking I learned there is no better way to really appreciate our beautiful country than to spend time on its magnificent waterways. You get an entirely different view of the countryside as you travel on a river.

But this was only one of many lessons I learned that I will talk about later in this book and that I hope may help you in your own unique journey in life. You never stop learning, and now, as older participants in our society, we have more time to learn. Now is the ideal time to pick up new skills and knowledge. Since turning sixty-five, I have taken lessons in fencing, fly fishing, rock climbing, trapezing, parachuting, tree surfing, snorkeling, Irish step dancing, welding. Recently, I even took a lesson in pole dancing.

Most of these experiences were exciting and broadening, making my life infinitely richer. Life is a trip in itself, a voyage with several stations along the way. This book is not only about my own voyage, it is about that journey of life, particularly in the later years. My purpose in writing it is to encourage and inspire you to be more adventuresome and enrich your own voyage through later years. It is never too late, and you are never too old, to do this. In fact, it's my firm conviction that you must seek some adventure in life in later years to complete your life voyage with health and satisfaction.

You are reading this book with a purpose. It may be beyond just hearing about an adventuring lady. Perhaps you too wish to use your senior years for trying new challenges, experiencing new facets of life. But again, maybe not. If you are content where you are, that's good. If your life is everything you want, that's fine. If you can go to your last reward and you are satisfied, more power to you. But ask yourself: Is there one thing you have always wanted to do but haven't done yet? Let that one thing pop into your head without forcing it, spontaneously. Maybe it's not snorkeling with sea lions in the Galapagos Islands or experiencing a night sandstorm in the Sahara Desert or jumping out of an airplane. But it will probably be something you hadn't thought of before. Your answer may even surprise you.

When I've asked this question of groups over the years, I've heard many surprises. One woman who lived on the outskirts of a big city reluctantly declared her break-out achievement would be to drive downtown by herself and park in a garage. That may seem simple to us, but it was an unclimbed mountain for her. Determined to conquer that mountain, she found a time when the traffic was light, and she drove downtown and parked by herself!

As another example, I once met a staid, matronly woman of the community, a banker's wife, whose great desire (one she called a secret) was to drive a semi-truck. She found a trucking company that was willing to let her climb in the cab and get behind the wheel of a big semi and drive around the parking lot. She accomplished her goal!

If there is one secret desire you have thought about in your quiet, solitary moments, I encourage you to accomplish it. As I have grown older and perhaps braver, my life has been ruled by the three Cs: Curiosity, Challenge, Change. Cultivate these qualities, and they can help you accomplish your unfulfilled goal and enrich your senior days with adventure, accomplishment, and satisfaction. Here they are in detail:

Curiosity—Be curious about everything. Ask questions, pursue the answers. At one time, I was a reference librarian, a position I loved. A library patron would come in with a question, and by the time we had discovered the answer and the patron had left the library, my curiosity would be aroused enough to look even further into the subject.

Challenge—Conquer rather than submit to problems and barriers in the road. If you live long enough, many challenges will hit you. The challenge may be health related (let's hope not) or family related, or it may be a self-proclaimed challenge. I do believe with the help of the Almighty and/or your angels, every challenge has an antidote.

Change—Be open to change. Life is full of alteration in the way things are, especially as we age. For some reason, not of your making, changes are flung at you, sometimes out of the blue. What? Your spouse announces after all these years he/she wants a divorce? Or, you need to move to a smaller house? Perhaps you are faced with the problem of a child who has lost a job and has nowhere to live—or worst of all, you do face a serious medical problem.

I don't want to alter your lifestyle. Well, maybe I do. I just want you to accomplish everything in life you want to do. Hopefully this book will help you put together your own to-do list, your rose-colored bucket list, a summary of your final life's ambitions. My daughter is a funeral director, and being that close to someone who takes care of others' final trips gives me a greater respect for life and a greater respect for everyday living. (Incidentally, I get a 15% discount.) Life is short, even if we live the maximum, so I encourage you to live every moment, every day, every year to the utmost. First envision, then find your adventure and DO IT!

This is a book of true stories, and the stories form the basis for discussion about adventure. They're about what I've done after the age of sixty, mostly after seventy. Each story is followed by tips to take you off on your own search for adventure. I hope to nudge you, I confess, out of your easy chairs in front of the TV and on to action.

The suggestions at the end of the chapter are in no way comprehensive or authoritative on the ideas I offer, however. I have tried to be as accurate as possible in listing agencies and opportunities for seniors, but some agency may quit listing its program the week after this book comes out. And who knows what experience you may have—it can be different from the one your neighbor has. Perhaps that's part of the intrigue of trying new things. What this book really offers are suggestions to stimulate your sense of adventure, and all of them in our home state.

Truthfully, I have been amazed at how many hundreds of chances there are in the state of Indiana today for seniors to strike out, experience intellectual or physical challenge, see different horizons, and discover intellectual or spiritual growth opportunities. My real wish is that you will find enjoyment in adventuring and make it a part of your life in these "golden olden years." Adventuring is a state of mind that lights up your moments and your days with anticipation and accomplishment. We are all meant to be active, to learn, and the years beyond family responsibilities and paid jobs provide great opportunities for action in life if we are alert to them.

One final word. Be very careful about assessing your own physical condition and ability for the more active adventures. I can't take any responsibility for what you do with these challenges. Still, I offer this wish for you after reading this book: stay fit, love life, and make each day count with love and laughter—and a dose of adventure.

Section 1: Envisioning Adventure

2
Being Adventuresome is Cultivated, but You're Also Born That Way Sometimes

Are you an adventurous sort of person? You don't need to be extremely "out of the box," eager for new experiences, venturesome, or even physically on the go all the time to be adventurous. All of us have within us the desire to find new paths, meet new people, and seek interesting happenings and experiences. That's why we go to see Indiana Jones movies and sign on for church or college trips to new places or even just attend an ethnic festival downtown. "Faraway places with strange-sounding names," do call us, even in a modest way. It's part of growing as we get older, and we need to grow always to live, to practice being curious, accepting challenges and welcoming change.

Still, some people are more adventuresome than others, ready for new challenges even from childhood. I was one of those. I was born in Chicago in the middle of the Depression. I'm sure adding another baby to the family was not on my parents' to-do list. The family moved to a small town along the Illinois River where I grew up in the 1940s. By "small town," I mean population 1,500. It was a safer environment than that of today and, typical of those different times, I could roam about the whole town on my used bicycle. I found that the most restful, quieting places in the world are on the water, and I enjoyed stopping to sit and watch that mighty Illinois roll by to join the Mississippi at Cairo. Living along the river must have made an impression because I came to appreciate water activities in later life.

My childhood was uneventful except for World War II whirling about me. I first heard the word "war" about 1942, when I was nine years old, and had to ask one of my fellow fourth-graders, "What's a war?" We soon found out. As a good Girl Scout, I went door-to-door collecting used grease to be utilized somehow for the war effort. There was a lot of rationing: gas, leather, sugar, and meat. My father ran a grocery store, so the rationing didn't affect me drastically, with the exception of shoes. Roving the neighborhoods as I did, I was very hard on shoes. My mother would caution me to not play so hard so I wouldn't wear out shoes so quickly. I never sat still. Mom would say, "I'll give you a nickel if you can sit still for five minutes." Big money in those days, but I never got that nickel. Although we didn't have these types of diagnoses then, I was probably a hyperactive kid, and I became a hyperactive old lady. If we are going to use curiosity as a focal point for the adventuring life, you can say I defined it: I was always ready for something around the bend.

My mother cautioned me a lot about stepping too far out of line. She had had a difficult life as a youngster. My brother and I knew little about her childhood, and most of her large family had died by the time I was interested in knowing. She didn't talk about her family life, and we didn't ask. I think she wanted to shelter me from life's disappointments. There was always a presentiment of secrecy that I couldn't decipher until she revealed that she had been married before and had two daughters. At the age of thirteen I suddenly found I had two half-sisters whom I never knew and unfortunately never really got to know. I vowed I would not keep secrets from my own children, which probably meant I blabbed at them too much. I also discerned that every child should be acknowledged and loved—never turned away. Later, I agreed to help raise a grandson. He was three when he came to live with me and I was sixty-five. I hadn't of course expected to take on this challenge, and it has been a challenge at times, but through prayers and tears, I've grown as a person through the experience and we are making it happen. If you are not open to change it will be thrust upon you.

Despite my mother's penchant for secrecy, she was a very good mother. She was also an innately intelligent woman who did a lot of reading, always visiting the library in our town as often as she could. I suspect her family was more intellectual than she ever disclosed.

She would take me to the library, and I discovered early that it was a wonderful place, especially for me with my eager mind. This small-town facility was a red brick Carnegie library with a lot of steps. Most Carnegie libraries in America still look like that. But it was magical to open the big oak doors, walk up ten steps to a landing, then another eight steps where I pushed my way through the large swinging doors. And there at the top of the stairs, sitting behind a huge, dark brown desk was the librarian! She seemed like the Wizard of Oz to me—the keeper of all the secrets in the world. And yes, she did say "Sshhh" a lot— her gray hair pulled back in a bun, the typical old-maid Guardian of the Books. But what she held in her hand was powerful: a yellow pencil with a little date stamp wrapped around the end of it, which she used to authoritatively stamp due dates in the back of books. I thought if I could ever have the power of this librarian, wielding that mystical yellow pencil to open all the doors of fantasy and adventure and knowledge in the world, I would have achieved Nirvana.

My father was from a stoic German family, and he never showed much emotion. He was a hunter and fisherman who never over-hunted or over-fished, an environmentalist of that day who truly loved the woods and outdoors, enjoying nature in all its forms. Coon hunting was the main activity in the fall. I went with him a few times and realized it took a lot of stamina to take part in chasing the coons. The coon hounds (at least one blue tick named Queenie) would be released in the woods, and the hunters would sit and wait until they heard the baying of those dogs. That meant the hounds had cornered a coon. Then the hunters would run (and I mean run) to the tree. As my father got older, he switched to fox hunting. In Illinois, fox hunting does not include riding horses across meadows and yelling "Tally-ho!" In Illinois, you took the foxhound to the woods and let him go. If your hound was good, he would bring the fox back to you where you were sitting—a lot less strenuous than coon hunting. Perhaps some people thought it was unusual for my father to take me, a girl, hunting with him from time to time, but that was what I wanted, and he obliged.

I liked school but felt I never fit in. I was different. My schoolmates may have felt that way, too. You know the old saying, "I wish I had a dollar for...."? Well, I wish I had one for every time I heard a classmate say about me, "Different! She always has to be different." I traveled my own path: Everyone ordered a class ring; I was the only one to order a class pin. Everyone went to the prom; I didn't want to go. Everyone ordered a yearbook; I did not. At that time I didn't take "different" as a compliment, but later I came to appreciate my uniqueness. In fact, I reveled in it.

I graduated from high school at age seventeen and went to work immediately as a secretary in a large corporation in Peoria. I really enjoyed the freedom of being a working girl for Caterpillar in the early 1950s—the Nifty Fifties. I bought swirly skirts and cashmere sweaters, wore high heels and little white gloves to work, fell in and out of love, and had a great time. I have always had a good sense of timing, knowing when it's the right time to do something. It came to me that it was time to marry and settle down and raise a family. I met my husband on a golf course and knew immediately I would marry him. After a year's courtship, we married, settling in Plymouth in northern Indiana, where we lived for forty years and raised four children. He was a good father and provided well, but he did have that natural instinct to control, so my adventurous spirit was kept in check for many years. It was lying dormant but grumbling, growling to be set free. Luckily I lived long enough to see that spirit of adventure take flight.

I, like my mother, enjoyed reading books, mostly nonfiction, so I educated myself without benefit of a degree. When I started college at a later age, I had already done a lot of self-educating.

I do believe having a role model is important in helping you achieve along new paths in life. I never thought I would become a role model, but think I seem to have become that in my late seventies, as a speaker who urges seniors to take control of their lives and live with as much adventure and excitement as they can cram in! Of course, I always admired Jenny Fields in *The World According to Garp*. In that novel Jenny writes a best-selling book encouraging women to do their own thing, and she is admired for her initiative and determination to help women—and to write about it. She may be a role model for me.

As a matter of fact, most of my role models would be women, the women of previous generations. Who knew they were doing extraordinary things? They didn't. They were just fulfilling what was expected of them at the time, which was a tremendous lot. I think men would still be sitting in Ohio in their covered wagons and the West would never have been won if it weren't for women. It was women who loaded everything in, got the children under the canvas top of the Conestoga and put them to work playing with their few home-made toys, then clambered up onto the buckboards and yelled, "Hitch up the horses and let's get goin'! It's time to cross the plains!"

My aunt worked for a wealthy family while she was in high school. She went on to earn a teacher's license and taught school until she married. Then she had to resign, because female teachers could not be married. As her family came along, she realized she needed to add to the family income. Aunt Bessie then worked full time six days a week in a department store. She would come home and fix meals, and every minute when she wasn't at her job or cooking, she would be canning fruits and vegetables from her big garden in the summer or cleaning the house, and incidentally putting her daughter through nursing school. After twenty years of work at the store, she went back to teaching, now that the rules had been changed. She taught in a one-room schoolhouse, and I was invited to accompany her there sometimes. She was the principal, teacher, janitor, counselor, truant officer, and playground superintendent. Obviously there was no teacher's union at that time. She even cleared the snow and ice from the front steps when winter weather set in.

I expect many of those reading this book are role models to friends and family, though they may not know it. Good advice for life is "Share your journey; don't hog it." After taking a speech class at Ivy Tech Community College, I feel as though I can speak in front of anyone and be mostly comfortable. It is only fair of me to share my journey and to encourage others to fulfill their dreams. When I started traveling, I didn't think I was on some kind of quest, but I guess I was. Now I am getting into that big world and sharing my stories, hoping they will inspire you to seek your own adventuring journey. You too can make living adventurously a truly rewarding part of the rest of your life! But first you must decide that you wish to "push out" in your life and put aside considerations that you are a senior and not "up to it." There are all kinds of adventures, and many of them are adventures of the will, heart, and mind. You must start by cultivating an adventuring state of thought, and that is done by envisioning a bright and active future in your senior years.

Tips:

First we must establish this fact: Our adventuring days are never "over the hill." I'd like to stimulate a desire for new experiences on your part. Do a brief memory writing piece, a letter if you will, to your children, grandchildren, or others: Pick out three adventures from childhood and describe them in detail. Give us the sights, smells, feelings. Then send copies to these people with any photos you have. This may whet your appetite for those bold experiences of your youth. It also could be the beginning of a valuable project of preserving your own heritage for those you care about and exploring the adventure of writing.

Do you read adventure books? Go to movies with high and fantastic adventure? Most of us like these. Perhaps we don't transfer to our own lives the state of mind that makes us enjoy seeing heroes or daring women solve mysteries, go to exotic lands, or undertake. But life itself is a quest, and once we overcome the idea that older people are sidelined and ought to sit still and be quiet watching others live, we can find our own rich and rewarding times.

Try an exercise: Imagine yourself on a bus to somewhere: a historical site, entertainment palace, or athletic dome. Think of a nice restaurant you would like to take in, the food on the table, the attractions in that spot, and the highlight of the trip, be it the awe of imagining the historic event or the quaint ambiance and charm of that place game, the excitement of the entertainment, or just the game. Project yourself socially. Envision your seat partner and think of a couple of conversation startups. Allow yourself to get excited about getting out into senior "Adventureland" in your mind. Then it will be possible to take the next step and implement.

Get over the idea that budget will hold you back. In our own neighborhoods and areas there are inexpensive or even free adventures that we can pursue. On local TV or in the city or county newspaper, watch for opportunities on the community calendar. If you are in a retirement community, check out the bulletin boards, but more importantly sign up.

Adventuring is a state of mind

Adventuring is a state of mind, but if you want to fill your life with new adventures, you should still be healthy enough do it! That is a part of life one should take care of on a daily basis. Exercise and eat right, especially lots of fruits and vegetables and modest portions of lean meats and whole grains. If you exercise enough you can work off a little bit of treat food. We all have to slip sometimes. I am slim, thanks to my slim father, but I do tend to eat too much unhealthy food at times. Right now my food fad is cheap fruitcake that I buy at the grocery store. In this I am a poor example. But I do stay fit. You can attend classes at a local fitness center or better yet, establish a routine of daily walking. It is amazing how much better our bodies feel after exercising. Statistics are showing that we could live to be 100 if we stay healthy and fit. Certainly succeeding generations will live to advanced ages.

3

Living in Two Worlds: A New Phase is Coming

Although I had never gone to college and sometimes felt circumscribed with the routine cares of the household, I had a husband who took care of the family and four interesting children. Still, I began to be aware even when the children were little that there was a very large world out there and I might enjoy living in it more fully one day. I came to have a restless desire to do more with my life. I wanted to step out of the box and try new things. Unfortunately, the message always was, "You can't do that." Or shouldn't. This was the mid-1960s, the beginning of the feminist movement, and I was the first in my small town to join NOW (at least mentally, as we didn't actually have a chapter in town). I will blame Betty Friedan for shaking me out of my comfort zone and making me think about my own future economic and financial needs, giving me permission to envision future excitement in life.

My two sons and two daughters eventually grew up, as children will do, and I began to realize that if that larger life I'd dreamed of was going to happen to me, I had to decide what it would be in detail and act. Nobody was going to help me fulfill my life but me. I began to allow myself to consciously consider, to envision, the active life I had yearned for all of these family years, one in which I would do some of the things I had wanted, but never received the encouragement to do. I realized I did not have the education my own children were achieving—a college education. I had only a high school diploma. College. That sounded glamorous and challenging and—fun. I would take just a course or two—maybe literature. I had always loved to read and had gobbled up the books in the Plymouth library. I made a call to Ancilla College near my hometown of Plymouth and began college.

I enrolled in that Catholic junior college at age forty-seven thinking I would take one class in literature. I was profoundly lucky to have as my first professor a nun who became my mentor. Sister Mary Dolores took me under her angelic wing and strongly encouraged me to continue my studies. She said, "You have to go on." And you do what the nun says, no matter your age or hers.

With her words ringing in my head, I plodded on, taking one class at a time, envying all those young people who had piled up credits I thought would be unattainable for me. My husband was from the "Me Tarzan, You Jane" school and did not approve of my going to college: a waste of time. After all, he would always take care of me. (Our roles were reversed later.) And speaking of waste, he wasn't going to waste any money to pay for my college education when I "should have done it earlier in life." So that meant I had to pay for it myself. I had a little money of my own that I had saved, and that would be the beginning of a personal Marie-only nest egg, one I could use to realize goals. I intended to build on that small financial basis for myself, not trusting to anybody else. And that is what I did.

I had some interesting experiences in college. In the first place, the students, some of whom had gone to high school with my children, didn't know what to call me as a classmate: Marie or Mrs. Albertson. Once I was in a sociology class, and the professor asked that we pair up to do a project. One very young female leaned across two desks and said to me, "I want to be your partner. You must have lived through everything!" I didn't think I had done that at the time.

I finally earned an associate's degree from Ancilla College in May 1983. Still hearing Sr. Mary Dolores urging me to continue, I enrolled at Indiana University in South Bend. I earned credits in different ways besides sitting in the classroom. By writing a thesis, I received credits for some of the volunteer work I had done over the years. I also signed up to work in security at the Pan Am Games in Indianapolis for credit. The first day, I was issued a badge with my picture on it. The next day, my badge was stolen. I couldn't figure out who would want to be wearing a badge with an old lady's picture on it, but it must have worked for someone, as it never showed up. The professor later questioned me about my stolen credentials but gave me the needed three credits.

As I worked for my bachelor's degree, my husband retired and contracted Parkinson's disease. I became a caretaker. Albert Schweitzer wrote, "Life becomes harder for us when we live for others, but it also becomes richer and happier." I had had some experience with taking care of someone before, with my mother. It was more difficult to care for my husband, who was slowly deteriorating. Parkinson's is an insidious disease; it moves at a snail's pace and takes many different turns that are enough to throw you off. Some days, he was good, and other days he was awful.

It was hard to work full time, continue with classes, keep the house, and take care of him. I was aware that in my generation and in this case of ours, it was a role reversal. You never know what lies in the future. I was employed as assistant librarian in the library in Plymouth, and I found myself rushing home to give him lunch, sometimes leaving my job when there was trouble, and spending my afternoons and evenings in care obligations. Of course I had made up my mind to do this out of love and responsibility; I wouldn't have him in a nursing home until it became really necessary, and when that did eventually happen, there were visits daily. And I began to take over the full management of the household: bill paying, upkeep, repairs and taxes, all those things he had done. Handling my own college education and husbanding the funds for it had put me in a confident position to take over all the financial obligations of the family, as well as everything else connected to family management in a house where there is a person who is gradually failing physically and mentally.

My husband got to the point where he should not be driving; however, since he had been driving for many, many years, he could not give it up. He was a traveling salesman, for heaven's sake. He drove every day, and as much complaining about his job as he did, he loved the freedom of driving off into the great beyond of salesmanship. Getting behind a wheel is the greatest feeling of independence. You are free behind that wheel! In good health, you can go anywhere, be anyone, but in bad health, it can be dangerous.

And dangerous it became one day when my husband found the car keys, which I thought I had hidden from him. Apparently, he had another pair stashed away. It was only one example of the kinds of unpredictable challenges that confront you with a devastating disease like Parkinson's. While working late one afternoon at the public library, I got a call from the local hospital. My husband had been in an accident and was being observed at the hospital. I rushed to the hospital and sat in the cold, cold waiting room. The medical staff had x-rayed every bone in his body, or so I thought. As we finally were wheeling him out the front door, one nurse said, "Oh, we didn't x-ray his nose." Why? Why would you x-ray his nose? If it is broken, what can you do? But he was wheeled back into the hospital and I was left waiting in that frigid waiting room.

The circumstances of the accident help show the irrational nature of these debilitating diseases that many of us will have to face for those close to us—or ourselves. There also has to be a moment of humor in our days, and this added that moment. It seems the reason my husband was doing forbidden driving was that he had a hankering for a strawberry milk shake from a McDonald's that is located on the other end of our town. He couldn't wait until I got home in less than two hours; he wanted his milk shake now! He got in his big Lincoln, drove north to McDonald's, and was heading home with his desired strawberry milk shake in his shaky hands. All of a sudden, between sips of his milk shake and watching the road, he must have lost control of his car, hit a parked pickup truck, bounced into the trunk of a huge, old tree, and then careened through a front yard where he came to a stop at the edge of someone's screened-in porch. Luckily, no one was home. Even luckier, although it was a school holiday and kids were strolling along the street where his accident occurred, thank the good Lord above, my husband missed the kids, hitting only inanimate objects.

When the ambulance arrived and EMTs helped him out of his totaled Lincoln, they spotted the red stuff splashed all over him, the blue leather dash, and the front window. What the EMTs mistook for blood was really his red strawberry milk shake. Too bad they didn't taste the "red stuff."

I guess you'd call it a good day: My husband wasn't injured, no schoolchildren were run over, and only his beloved Lincoln had met its match that day. I was able to bring him home in one piece. It was just another day in the life of a caregiver. Do not let anyone besmirch the lives of caregivers; they belong in a special place in Heaven.

But through all of the caretaking years I never lost sight of my goals. There would come a time in the near future when my duties would be done, leaving me with sadness, resignation, and yet expectation in equal parts. It was obvious a different life pattern was coming. I would have a career and some adventures when these responsibilities were finished. Preparing for that life was almost as important as making my husband comfortable in his last days. So all during this time, I continued going to school. I graduated from IUSB with a bachelor's degree in liberal arts in May 1988.

But why not go on farther in my education? I planned to take eighteen of the thirty-six needed credits for a master's degree. That would be enough of an education, wouldn't it? However, I got halfway through and thought, why not finish? And that is what I did. After thirteen years of attending college classes, I earned a master's degree in library science at age sixty. It's never too late!

My education and envisioning a new life was happening as my husband was winding down, two processes at once, and I am glad I had the foresight to live in the two worlds, present and future at once. I believe I was able to give my full attention as needed to my husband of forty years. Still, I did save a portion of my time and thinking for the future. That was not disloyal; it was the right things to do. Perhaps that illustrates the use of the three principles I advised for you, too: curiosity, acceptance of challenge, and openness to change. I didn't recognize that pattern or filter out any list of guiding principles at that time, but looking back I can see I had to be courageous and open, thinking realistically about the future as I did the most loving job I could in the present.

First I had to consider work, gainful employment, when my days as a caretaker were over. I had a college education now, with an advanced degree. So I could probably get a decent librarian's job. But where? Did I want to stay in the same town after my children were out and away living their own lives? Three had left town by this time, and it seemed obvious the other might at some point. Beyond that, could I dare to say there were places I wanted to go, things I wanted to see, experiences I should savor in the years remaining? Wouldn't some of those puritanical neighbors look down their noses at me? I could just hear it—"Why are you thinking beyond? Your full attention should be on your husband right now." Thinking practically about the future in times of trouble requires courage and openness to change!

I made a mental list, more of a plan, and looked at all sides of my realistic visions for the future:

Career: So I would be employed after my husband was gone. I had to envision salary and workplace, realistic objectives for someone who could work as a librarian for maybe ten years. I was not going to end up, after all, as head librarian at the Library of Congress.

Travel: Where did I want to go? Who would I go with? What will the level of my expectations be? How will I pay? That was especially important.

Adventuring: There was so much out there, so many places a person in good health and with a little money, some travel brochures, and a lot of excitement could go. I'd been such an adventuresome child. I wanted to rediscover that me. I was thirsty for experience after so many years of subordinating myself. Would I learn to canoe or kayak? Get into a fitness program? Try some really venturesome experiences like parachuting? It was all ahead of me, and I listed goals

I wanted to achieve, planned, and then made decisions.

I'd like to say that the need to plan, to envision the next phase of life and include in that planning the thought of adventuring doesn't just apply to caregivers or people facing gloomy changes. Those retiring from a full work life are most open to thoughts of adventure, be it in a trailer at Jupiter Beach in Florida or a cabin in the northwoods of the Upper Peninsula of Michigan, starting a new business built on skills of the long work life, or developing musical skills that have been latent since high school by joining the performing band in your area. We all can envision and then—do it!

What can I share about this for you? This is the first set of over two hundred tips I'll be giving you at the end of the adventuring stories in this book.

Tips:
Caregiving affords you a rare opportunity to not only learn about patience and giving, to love as fully as you can, and to be realistic about finances and getting help but also to realize there will be a time when you must forge a life of your own. Plan and act decisively during the wind-down process! The same thing goes for retiring from a life on the job as you may think about owning your own small business or consulting service. Give yourself two years of planning and make adventuring in all kinds of ways a top priority.

Decisions about the future when a spouse or other person on whom you depend is gone can happen for other reasons and may come suddenly: change of circumstances, divorce, or reversal of fortune may make us have to think about the future. At that time, even if it occurs unexpectedly, realize amidst your other adjustment strategies that you have an opportunity for a new and exciting phase of life! It will help compensate for the usually unwelcome change you are experiencing and give you positive energy for coping and new life.

Realize that there are adventuring opportunities within almost every budget, and realistically assess your ability and the chances that are out there. Specifically research your area's educational opportunities, arts and culture and sporting offerings, many for free or low cost if your budget is limited. Make a specific "rose-colored bucket list" and keep it in a special place. It's about planning in advance.

I also recommend becoming a saver. I was trained as a kid to save, save, save. When I got married, I realized my prior saving habits came in handy because my husband made a good living as a salesman and he liked to spend money. There cannot be two spenders in one family, so I became the saver. If you are going to envision a future beyond your family or caretaking years, as I did, you are going to have to cultivate enough independence to carry on by yourself. If you have not learned to pay the bills, learn to do so, either by old-fashioned signing of checks or by utilizing Internet banking systems. Begin paying off bills that will hamper you and start saving, no matter how small the amounts. Be aware of what will be coming to you in the way of any investments or social security and obligations you will have as years unfold. Think about a part-time job, whatever that may be for your skills or experience. If more extensive travel or educational choices are on your horizon, consult your financial advisor.

Don't necessarily ask the advice of your children or close relatives as you make your plans for "the rest of your life." Develop your strategy and lists and then share your wishes with them. This is your life, and they may have reservations about your plans for one reason or another. You can show them you can master a new phase of living by actually doing it.

Physically challenged or in less-than-perfect health? Consider small adventures with transportation provided and handicapped-accessible facilities. Consult your events director or local library, which stands ready to help with activities for handicapped people. Ask about public or private transportation. Make calls to the local restaurant or arts center and ask what provisions they have for those who have limited mobility. Every day can include adventuring if living fully and blessing others is the goal of life.

TRY THIS OUT: EXERCISES IN ADVENTURING

Look at this list just once and see if any of these things have come to as things you might have wanted to do "in the future." If you react with a "yes," put a check by the item:

o Travel with a grandchild or other relatives on a trip near or far

- Get a part- or full-time job, maybe growing out of your previous experience but maybe not!
- Write a novel or memoir
- Take a class at the local senior center, library, or extended education center
- Join a group connected with your interests. Military veteran? Handcrafting? Book group? History or genealogy?
- Develop musical or dancing talent left behind years ago now just for fun
- Learn to scuba dive
- Become a lay or even full-time minister in your faith group
- Buy and learn to use a computer
- Get active in your sorority, fraternity, church group, or civic action group

These and many more ideas will be explored in the rest of the chapters, but thinking of these popular interests can get you started.

What's a Nice, Mild-mannered Librarian Like Me Doing in a Mess Like This?

My husband was gone. I'd said goodbye with dignity and appreciation to all the good memories, children shared, and a home built. Now here I was living in a strange city looking for a new job at age sixty-three! I had envisioned work growing out of my training and the town in which my children had grown up. My secure position as an assistant director in a small library in a small town wasn't good enough. I had to leave it all behind, take a leap of faith into the big city like Indiana Jones when he steps into an abyss and finds a sturdy step. I had relied on that faith but found that the first step was a bit slippery. I can tell you, Indiana Jane I wasn't!

After cleaning out a five-bedroom house full of forty years of collected memorabilia, I loaded up my little car in the middle of a January snowstorm and headed south to Indianapolis. The car was so full I couldn't see out of my rearview mirror. When I looked to the back of my car, though, I felt my angels were with me. I could feel their presence and felt the warmth of their approval. So I knew I was doing the right thing at the right time. I had always been a late bloomer, so I told myself I was doing some more late-in-life flowering.

Interestingly, I never asked my grown children's advice. It never occurred to me. They had been not only dear children but friends, and I had consciously worked at having them close in my life. But they weren't going to be asked to give an opinion on this big change in my life. This was my life; I would not be asking anything of them except whatever love and support they could give me as part of our lives. I had to chart my own course.

I eventually found a small house that seemed just right for me.

When I started my job quest, I was filled with confidence. After all, I had a master's degree on my resume: what could stop me now? So, I wasn't twenty years old and did have a mop of grey hair—that surely wouldn't make a difference. At least I thought it wouldn't until my first interview. The interviewer, who looked to be about twelve, leaned across the desk and asked, "How much longer do you plan to work?" There were a few more unsatisfactory interviews—even one at a temp agency where I flunked a typing test. I had only been typing for about fifty years. This job hunting was not looking good. Would I have to go back to the small town and admit defeat? The idea seemed bleak and dismal.

I finally secured an interview at the Indiana State Library. The interview went fairly well, but I wasn't sure I would be offered the job. As I left the interviewer said, "We'll let you know." That's an iffy phrase. Thinking about it, I decided that I might be having a problem with my gray hair. I stopped at a busy hair salon and almost shouted to the first available stylist, "Dye my hair." The stylist was a smoker, so after applying all the magic colored gook on my head, she went out back for a cigarette break. I sat in the chair, hair wrapped in a towel, for what seemed like an awful long time. She finally remembered me, came running through the back door, whipped off the towel and voila! I had maroon hair—think Cordovan shoe polish maroon. I couldn't believe it. This was something I certainly hadn't envisioned back in the planning days.

As I drove home, I often glanced in the mirror, still unable to believe my hair color. When I walked in the door, I had a message from the Indiana State Library. I was offered the position in the library's development office. Oh happy day!

When I joined the library office the next day, my boss probably wondered what happened to the grey-haired lady she had interviewed the day before. She never ever mentioned my hair. And neither did I.

Maroon hair and all, when I was hired at the Indiana State

Library, I was overjoyed. Actually, that was hardly the word for it. I was consumed with happiness. I thanked God and my angels for this wonderful "promotion" in life.

The Indiana State Library was constructed in 1934 and is a beautiful building, inside and outside. This stately classical building sits on the corner of Senate and Ohio Streets in Indianapolis. I became so enthralled with the building; I would give guided tours to schoolchildren. Guided tours are available most days, and I recommend you make a visit if you have not when you are downtown. If you enter on the Senate Street entrance, the first thing you will see is the marble staircase that leads up the main lobby. The lobby contains large stained-glass windows, and in the afternoons the sun streams through the windows, filtering beautiful colored magic lantern lights onto the stone floor. On each side of the foyer, scenes of Indiana history are painted on the walls. These large paintings help any Hoosier appreciate the state's history: Indian treaties, Revolutionary War scenes, farm life.

When I started at the library, I was so joyous about securing a library position in this marvelous building that my enthusiasm was sometimes misunderstood. In all my happiness I was literally skipping down the long hallways. The other librarians did not understand why I was so happy. They hadn't been yearning for a job like I had for most of my adult lifetime. I actually wanted to start a skipping club, but that didn't go over very well.

The other librarians were friendly and helpful. My office was on the fourth floor, providing a panorama of the city. Through the large window (which actually opened) in my cubicle, I was able to look out on a green lawn below and across the street to the stately late nineteenth-century Indiana Capitol building on Senate Avenue. All I had to do was stand and take in all the sounds and sights of the big city to give myself inspiration each day. How lucky could a girl get! The job part of the envisioning and planning had paid off.

I was hired as a full-time consultant in the development office working with literacy, physically handicapped patrons, and institutional libraries around the state. I enjoyed the work, especially working with the librarians at institutions such as mental health facilities and schools for the developmentally challenged. When I visited the Indiana prisons, I met with prison librarians and also some of the offenders who worked as assistants in the libraries. When I say libraries, I could mean either four shelves or a whole room, depending on the prison and its operators. My first visit to one of these institutions caused me some apprehension, but the prisons for which I had responsibility were considered medium security. If there were maximum-security offenders, they were not in the area I visited.

On one of these typical visits, I would arrive having made previous arrangements with the prison librarian so he/she would inform the staff in the front lobby to expect me. I would be welcomed and screened for admittance. There were some restrictions: I could not carry matches or money into the prison areas, not even into the libraries. My handbag was kept at the front desk until I returned. While waiting for the librarian, I would meet and talk with some of the offenders who worked in the library. To work in the library was considered the best job in the prison, so most of these men and women were thought to be responsible. They were generally well spoken, curious, and ready to work. At the women's prison I was surprised to discover what pride they took in themselves, looking for all the world like sorority girls, their hair fixed beautifully with the aid of the prison beauty shop. And you have no idea how many times I heard, "I am innocent."

On my initial visit to any one prison, the librarian would take me around the prison area and introduce me to some of the other workers. At one facility, we sat in the cafeteria and had lunch—it was a sunny, pleasant day, and as I looked out through the rolled, barbed-wire fence I came to appreciate freedom. It gives a person a different feeling when he or she knows he can walk out into the sunshine and enjoy freedom with few restrictions. One of the things about breaking out of the mold when you are a senior citizen is that you can reflect on life, your own and the entire process. What is precious comes to the forefront; what is not as important as you once thought falls away.

The senior years are also an opportunity in one's job to exhibit creativity based on the confidence born of experience and the desire to do some good things while you have the chance. I made it a duty for my position at the state library to collect unwanted books from the Indiana public libraries and ship or haul them to the prison libraries. They were always short on books and money. I was also in charge of applying for grants for the prison libraries to help these useful little services obtain needed resources. We contributed fiction, romance, biographies, and thrillers. One of their favorites was *The Da Vinci Code.* Several of the libraries had law books, and I remember seeing some of the prisoners hunched over, studying these books intently. I came to believe through these experiences that the way to reduce recidivism is through education. The library could be a good place to start that process. Most prisons had vocational training, as well.

I had a much-appreciated opportunity to create a project of my own, to put a stamp on the types of values I had brought into the job and believed I could contribute to the library and our state's program. In my position I received many new children books from publishers, probably overruns, but in excellent shape. With the encouragement of my boss and working with the prison librarians, I created a "Read To Me" program for the offenders. I would provide the children's books and a cassette tape. The chosen offenders would read and record the books, then send the book and tape back to me. The library would cover the cost of postage to send the book and the tape to the offender's child. In addition, with the help of a video expert in our office, we were able to videotape the women at the Indiana Women's Prison reading the books to their children. Over 80 percent of the incarcerated women were mothers, and the women I met were under thirty years of age. Almost all the female offenders were jailed because of transporting addictive products for someone else.

The program was successful and in fact caught the eye of a national reporter. *The Wall Street Journal* called me and wanted some facts about the Read program. We were subsequently mentioned in an article on the front page of the *Journal*. More importantly, I received many letters from the offenders praising the program and detailing what it meant to them. It opened a line of communication with their children and helped them have something in common to talk about during their limited phone conversations. One young male offender wrote, "It gave me a reason to go home." The women were especially appreciative. One young mother, whose mother was keeping her child during her years in prison, wrote, "When my mother plays the video on our TV, my daughter hugs the TV."

When I reached the age of seventy, I decided it was time to retire from the Indiana State Library. The powers that be at the State House offered retirees an added bonus if they left in 2003. It wasn't a big chunk of cash since I had only worked there for seven years, but it was enough to push me off into the seat of rocker retirement. I definitely knew there would be no rocker in my retirement future anyway. My list was long and mostly unfulfilled, and the years stretched ahead. I enrolled in a counseling program at Ivy Tech with the idea of working with older women, to encourage and inspire them to create more adventurous lifestyles. When I graduated with an associate's degree in counseling, I made all my grandchildren attend the commencement, thinking they would get some idea of what can be accomplished at an older age. Afterward, I asked one of them what she thought, and she said, "Gee, that was boring." And I replied, "Yeah, I've attended lots of your boring stuff, too." Dancing recitals and high school graduations come to mind. (I'm such a wonderful grandmother!)

But it was definitely time to move on into the rest of my "Envisioning Adventure" list. My mantra was: A woman should experience everything in life she can afford—and some things she can't afford. I was about to put that to the test.

Travel was tops on that adventuring planning list. Now I had to implement the dreams, make the visions come to life.

    As a part of my adventuring agenda while I was still at the library, I had learned how to kayak at age sixty-five. I had enjoyed kayaking on many rivers in the western U.S. and on the east coast and met many interesting campers and kayakers. At night we would sit around the campfire and my fellow campers talked about the traveling they had done or were planning to do. A few had been around the world. Many of them talked about traveling overseas, abroad, on the continent. Wait a minute! I thought I was a well-rounded traveler exploring the rivers in the U.S. I felt like a travel virgin compared to all their wonderful journeying. I promised myself when I got the time and the opportunity to explore the world, I would do it, too. So when I said goodbye to the library, I prepared to "do the world." I determined to travel and visit every continent on the planet. That would be my specific goal.

    After I completed my studies, I took off to my first trip—walking on the Great Wall—the first of my travel fantasies.

    Tips:
Even as you work in full-time employment, in those last years when you are realistically closing down your work and leaving the office to the young upstarts, set goals for the next phase and make them specific. Consider people to reintegrate into your life, destinations, educational programs to pursue, groups or clubs to join or rejoin, a small business to start up or develop, volunteer programs to investigate, and then do it. You have cousins you haven't seen in years and now wished you could catch up with? Older years are great for "cousining."

    By necessity or desire you may be working beyond the normal age retirement. If this is your desire, you may be able to convince your place of work that having your experience on the job will continue to enhance the business, or you may apply somewhere else, emphasizing your wisdom and work ethic. There are places that will value these qualities, though it may take time to find them. Initiate a large job search, possibly showing up in person, and don't give up until you get something interesting. In today's economy part-time employment is everywhere and attractive to managers of businesses. Here is where the adventuring factor comes in: you may wish to try something you'd never have dreamed, something venturesome, people-oriented, or unusual. Present yourself and it may be yours.

After you've discovered how the system works at your place of employment, dare to innovate. Find the right friend to help you develop a new program, gain a goal for the company or agency, or create something to make workers' lives more fun or easier. That's the sense of adventure we've been talking about—right in the office.

Pay careful attention to any retirement benefits or financial opportunities. Even if you have only a limited time to work, there are parts of plans that may give you much-needed income to supplement your Social Security payments.

Teaching a class as an adjunct professor at the community college or university branch in your town is a good working opportunity after you close down full-time employment. The pay is modest, but the intellectual opportunity is real! What do you know about as a work specialty, hobby, or special interest? You may teach it in a community learning center. The subject matter is wide and depends only on your own knowledge and expertise, from health to Bible study courses to cooking specialties to gardening—you get the idea. Call your local community college, library, church office, or volunteer or senior citizen agency and offer to enrich their programs through your own lecturing or teaching. Some of these teaching or lecturing opportunities offer honoraria or pay and travel expenses. Some seniors have developed a second career in appearing before groups or teaching classes.

And remember, volunteering in your own neighborhood is a serious job. All of the above areas of adventuring and being paid in a worthwhile job can be employed in a volunteer setting. Be sure you thoroughly investigate the volunteer program of whatever agency you are interested in to see if volunteers feel rewarded and happy in their jobs. Again, look for the adventure in the volunteer experience. Face the huge jumping carp at the conservation center pond as you guide schoolchildren around, learn a new skill at operating the boat at the state park, revive your long-lost skill in spinning for the farm museum or knowledge of painting by serving as a docent at the art museum. You can learn to lead and teach and be comfortable with people even if you have not thought of those as your skills. Step right up! What have you wanted, longed to do? You can do it now.

The Indiana State Library is only one of our Hoosier state historical resources that can qualify as easily accessible adventures to investigate and they serve multiple purposes in our discussion here because they hire part time, need volunteers, and provide visiting adventures. The Eugene and Marilyn Glick Indiana History Center, 450 W. Ohio Street, Indianapolis, houses the Indiana Historical Society and has interactive exhibits ranging from Prohibition in the Hoosier State to the Underground Railroad, all lively and interesting. They are interested in both part-time hiring and volunteer assistance, too. Conner Prairie in Noblesville has been named the most outstanding interactive history center in America, and you can experience an interactive visit with costumed pioneers in either the frontier village or the later farm village. The 1859 balloon voyage takes you high above the countryside and is a qualified high adventure. Conner Prairie welcomes volunteers of all sorts, from playing the pioneer blacksmith dressed in period dress to helping in the ticket booth. Ft. Wayne has reopened the Old Ft. Wayne reenactment center, and the Fulton County Historical Society has a dandy late-nineteenth-century village set up right on its grounds on US 31. These examples will stand for only a few of the many historical villages throughout the state that provide intellectual and sometimes physical adventures as well opportunities for volunteering and sometimes part-time work. They're family fun, too.

As far as the state of Indiana goes, its historical sites are crowned by the Indiana State Museum, 650 W. Washington Street in Indianapolis, considered to be the best state museum in the country, with its re-creation of the tearoom in the L. S. Ayres department store and the gallery of famous Hoosiers. Two other favorites are the Territorial Capitol in Vincennes and the first state capitol at Corydon. And while you are adventuring there in southern Indiana, you can travel to see the site of the only Civil War battle fought in Indiana—the Battle of Corydon. Let yourself imagine the troops of Morgan the Raider are coming at you as you wait with the other local volunteers, squirrel rifles at the ready, behind the bulwarks, here comes the Confederate cavalry—and then you run. Hooray! Once you have visited, you can decide on volunteering or part-time work options. Visit, volunteer, or work.

Section II
Adventuring Through Travel

5

Destination: China

Curiosity, one of the Three Cs, stimulates our thinking, keeps us focused on the future, and revitalizes our life as seniors. Studies have even shown curiosity is one of the qualities that helps develop positive health. There are many ways to satisfy curiosity, but getting out of the house, apartment, or living center is one of the best ways. Be it to the next town for the best cheeseburger around and a look at the small museum dedicated to the town's history or a trip far away, travel keeps us young in our minds and hearts. Still working and volunteering? Traveling can be a part of your life during this time, too.

The articles in this section chart my own course as I broke out of the box and took the trips I'd planned in my mind as I was caretaking and envisioning the next phase of my life. My travel happened both as I was working in my senior employment opportunity at the library, when I traveled in the U.S., and later, when I was retired and headed for international travel.

Let's start with the first worldwide trip I took: to China, to the Great Wall, February 2006. Nothing like starting big!

As a kid in a small town in central Illinois gazing at pictures of the Great Wall in China, visiting it in person seemed an impossible dream. Even as I read about the Great Wall later in life as a librarian, it didn't occur to me as a realistic possibility. One fortunate day, I stumbled across information about a trip to China offered by a local travel company. Would my first trip abroad be to China and the Great Wall? It was a long way away, and the costs seemed too high for my modest circumstances. The trip several years ago was more than $4,000 for nineteen days of sightseeing all over China; however, there was one line that caught my eye—a person could go on the trip and stay in Beijing for half the price. That seemed more within my budget. The best part was that the Beijing-only trip included a side sojourn to the Great Wall! I had to go. Gathering my adventurous spirit, I called and signed up. I attended the first information meeting and was introduced to the young guide from the travel bureau. There were just a few people at this meeting, but we were told that the others would join us later.

On the day of departure, I threw my packed suitcase in the trunk, drove to the airport, parked, and went inside the terminal. What I was expecting was a group of people welcoming me to be part of a large traveling contingent to the Far East, or at very least, the young guide holding a big CHINA sign in her hand. What I found was that few people were even in the airport at that hour—I always get there early—and no one even looked as though they were excitedly going to board a plane and fly eastward for 13.5 hours. I was beginning to think I had the wrong day. Finally, the young guide showed up. I was thankful to recognize her, and I reintroduced myself. She said one other person would be on the flight with me. It turned out the other woman who would be on the same plane had made this trip numerous times. She informed me she had filled up several passports not only because her daughter was living and attending school in Beijing, but because she had been around the world. I reluctantly admitted that China would be the first stamp in my virgin passport.

The nonstop flight from Chicago to China was very long. I cannot sleep on a plane, so I can tell you it was exceedingly long. We landed in Beijing in late evening. The sky was grey, and the traffic from the airport was unbelievably heavy. We met our Chinese guide and fellow travelers at the hotel—about sixteen of us in all and mostly couples. I was so excited about actually being in China I didn't mind traveling alone, plus I had a great room to myself in a beautiful, upscale hotel in downtown Beijing.

The well-versed guide took us around to all the sights in the city—the usual sights: Tiananmen Square, the Forbidden City where the emperors lived, and many museums. China was preparing for the Olympics in two years from that time, so we were able to view the unfinished Olympic Village and the impressive building that came to be known as the Bird's Nest. One day we boarded a bus and traveled northwest to the Great Wall. I was so excited! I was going to fulfill my lifelong dream of actually being at, and walking on, the Great Wall of China! And it was worth all the money I spent to get here. What a thrill!

We arrived at the area where we would climb the steps and walk on that wall, created beginning in the seventh century BC by warlords and improved through many dynasties, 8,851 kilometers or 5,500 miles in length. After I practically flew out of the bus, I discovered to my dismay that my camera didn't work. Luckily the area had many consumer-enticing shops, and one sold a one-use camera. Finally, many steep steps later, I was at last stepping on the Great Wall. The walking area is narrow and made of irregular stones with low walls and often a steep drop-off. Although the weather was cloudy and grey, I could see the wall winding ahead and behind me for what seemed to be miles. Turrets were placed every mile or so to spot invading tribes and warn the countryside with smoldering fires. This "giant dragon" stretching across the land is always in need of repair on some of its walls, but considering it was built two thousand years ago, it is still a marvelous spot to visit.

Back in Beijing, all of the other travelers were going to the interior of China, which meant I would be in the city by myself. A fellow librarian in Indiana, originally from China, had told me about a classmate she had in Beijing. She made arrangements with her friend, Janet, to meet me in the hotel lobby. Janet turned out to be delightful and spoke beautiful English. She was a busy career woman who took time from her schedule to show me other, less well-known sights of Beijing. She introduced me to a lot of local customs, and we visited the oldest areas of the city. We were in and out of taxis, and at one point an interesting heated exchange began between Janet and the driver—all in Chinese of course.

Later, at the airport while leaving Beijing, I had difficulty getting past a security woman who kept telling me I had some contraband in my suitcase. I finally convinced her I was clean. The plane ride home challenged my view of travel as a friendship-building experience. After the plane took off, the man next to me passed gas, passed gas again, then accepted a bowl of soup to put on his tray and promptly went to sleep, allowing the soup to spill on me.

In the confusion at security in the Beijing airport, I had taken off my jacket and mistakenly left it there. After my return I told my librarian friend about leaving my jacket behind. Without my encouragement, she contacted Janet in China. Janet drove to the huge international airport in Beijing, found my jacket, and mailed it to me. I will never get over her thoughtfulness. Janet's kindness was a wonderful conclusion to my first trip to a foreign land. You never know when new views of how good people are will be one of the unexpected benefits of travel.

Tips:

Patience on trips to places in the far corners of the world is useful. Take a book or two that you just can't put down. DVD? Tapes or audiobooks? This is the time to use that new Kindle your grandchildren gave you for Christmas.

Don't expect glossy travel brochure experiences every day, complete with perfect arrangements, photogenic natives, and superb weather. Less-than-perfect experiences calling for you to improvise can help round out your travel memories.

Always carry extra batteries for your camera or an extra "emergency" camera—or develop the ability to take photos with your smartphone.

When staying at a hotel, check to see if they offer Internet access. Every night send an email to yourself describing what happened that day. Or make arrangements with a teacher for you to send to his/her class vivid descriptions of your trip.

Cash Conscious?

Group travel companies often have bargain slots in their itineraries, perhaps at the last minute. This you arrange by phone or email. Search the Internet and ask the travel agent in advance what types of bargains are offered at certain times. They probably won't volunteer this information.

There can also be a discount from a service you render (Give a talk? Lead a writing or cooking or language class? Entertain?), or you may earn your way completely by taking some responsibility on the trip. Elderhostel (now called Road Scholar) has in my experience been willing to let you go to their wonderful programs free if you raise a group of eight to ten friends and stand as their chaperone.

Road Scholar has trips around the U.S. in the $400-$700 range for four or five nights with meals. Seniors can now take along a grandchild on some of these trips. The destinations and learning experiences on these inexpensive trips can immerse you in opera or Bach, or set you up to build a Heifer Village. A favorite trip of mine is visiting Cahokia and, with an experienced archaeologist, climbing Monks Mound and re-experiencing the Mound Builders' culture of a thousand years ago. Visit http://www.road-scholar.com/.

6

Destination: Alaska

My goal was to visit every continent, and I had found a good starting place with China. Now I began thinking about the North American continent. When I discovered a reasonably priced trip to Alaska, I couldn't resist. Those cheap seats are always too much for me to pass up, and I had always wanted to see Alaska. So in September 2007 I made the trip north.

After traveling alone and experiencing some delays, I arrived in Sitka, Alaska. There are only two ways to get to Sitka—either by air or boat. (It was interesting to later see Sitka school kids waiting in the airport for their flights. The sports teams have to fly to compete.) We arrived at the airport late at night, and that was a good thing after I saw, in the daylight, the small landing strip that juts into Sitka Sound.

Feeling stranded in the small Sitka airport (which would probably close soon) in a strange city proved to be a bit disquieting. For the first time I felt apprehensive about traveling alone. I had no idea where the lodge was, and there was no one in the airport with open arms to welcome the lone tourist from Indiana. What should I do? Luckily I noticed a couple who looked as perplexed as I did. Although I hadn't realized it, they had been on the same plane and tour, and they too were looking for our lodging. We found a lone taxicab in the parking lot. Sitka can be very dark at night, but the taxi driver found our lodge, which was nestled among the trees along the Sitka Sound. We stumbled into the place while the other ten tour members were sound asleep.

Sitka, an old fishing village, receives more than ninety inches of rainfall a year. The town backs up to mountains to the east, so any moisture coming off the Pacific gets dumped on the town before it hits the mountains. We were introduced to a guide who, like most of the guides for my travels, turned out to be competent and personable. She loved her town and was well versed in all it had to offer. As we trudged through Sitka's temperate zone rain forest, replete with drooping vines, our guide pointed out all the wildlife that my untrained eyes could not discern, including a big yellow banana slug, which was intriguing as long as it stayed on the moss-covered trees. We also explored the waters in Sitka Sound, which contains more than two hundred small islands.

One day we boarded a small boat to sail into the sound and saw a family of orca whales, including a black and white baby, leaping over the waves, enjoying family life and the choppy water. Our guide spotted an Alaskan brown bear (which was black) sitting on shore having a feast with all the spawning salmon. The bear speared one fish after another with his big paw, chomped off a head, tossed the headless fish aside, and dipped into the water for another fish. I learned the bears want the oily substance in the heads of the fish, which builds up fat for them during their winter hibernation.

The weather was amazingly gracious; even the natives were excited about our wealth of sunshine. We kayaked in the rough waters of Sitka Sound and hiked to the top of the mountains behind the town. It was a glorious experience looking over the beautiful blue sound and then turning to see the magnificent snow-covered mountains miles and miles to the north toward Anchorage. We can never tire of beauty, and when new phases of beauty come to us after we think we've seen everything, it thrills us and gives us plenty to talk about and remember, both good things—also "photo ops."

After ten days in Sitka, I flew to Anchorage, and as I waited for my plane on another sunny day, I walked around the town, soaking up some of its gold-rush history. I have always been a fan of the poet Robert Service, so I searched for the place for his local poetry but was unable to locate any scenes. Taking another city bus back to the airport, I discovered much of Alaska's wildlife (human in this case) is on the city bus system. The forty-ninth state is truly a beautiful, interesting area and should be on everyone's travel list.

Just a generation back, a woman traveling alone without a man would have been a bit suspect. Times have changed. I was not afraid to travel alone on my several trips, in spite of moments of fear in the Sitka airport. A family story came to mind when I considered being a solitary lady on a trip. One of the few tales my mother told me about her mother had to do with "womaning up" alone. My grandmother, whom I never met, took my mother and one of her young sons to North Dakota in the early 1900s to homestead all by herself. She left her husband in Illinois and built a sod house in the fall so she and her young children could live in it during the harsh winter on the Great Plains. She claimed she was a widow; government land grants went only to widowed, unmarried, or divorced women. Homesteaders had to live on their land in order to claim it as theirs. It all sounded exciting, no doubt. Eventually they all returned to Illinois, their foray into homesteading over. Apparently adventurous women were always in my family tree.

Off and on I kept notes as a sort of informal travel journal, and I wish I had written down even more of my journeys. That is a fine way to continue your spirit of adventure long after the plane touches down. You will be continually busy on whatever trip you elect to take (next town or around the world), but do take the time in the evening to jot down your thoughts, impressions, and insights. And of course take photos with your camera or cellphone and remember—put people in them. Nobody, not even you, wants to look through your photos a couple of years from now and see a bunch of mountains or a boat far away on the horizon with no real interest anymore. And perhaps instruct your photo subjects not to look at the camera but to be doing something interesting.

Robert Service was one of the great adventurers of all time in Alaska. The poem *The Face on the Barroom Floor* has been attributed to him but it isn't by him. I was thinking about that face, though, when I searched for the barroom the poet wrote about.

> *'Twas a balmy summer evening and a goodly crowd was there*
> *Which well-nigh filled Joe's barroom on the corner of the square,*
> *And as songs and witty stories came through the open door*
> *A vagabond crept slowly in and posed upon the floor.*
> *"Where did it come from?" Someone said. "The wind has blown it in."*
> *"What does it want?" another cried, "Some whisky, rum or gin?"*
> *"Here, Toby, seek him, if your stomach's equal to the work—*
> *I wouldn't touch him with a fork, He's as filthy as a Turk."*
> *This badinage the poor wretch took with stoical good grace;*
> *In fact, he smiled as though he thought he'd struck the proper place.*
> *"Come, boys, I know there's kindly hearts among so good a crowd—*
> *To be in such good company would make a deacon proud."*
> *"Give me a drink—that's what I want—*
> *I'm out of funds, you know;*
> *When I had cash to treat the gang, this hand was never slow.*
> *What? You laugh as if you thought this pocket never held a sou:*
> *I once was fixed as well, my boys, as anyone of you."*

Tips:

If you feel deserted or confused when stranded in a strange place, it's desirable to ask a lot of questions and keep yourself from panicking. If you keep cool, you can make it part of the travel experience. Adjusting to sudden changes and misunderstandings is all part of the adventure of solo traveling, and you can build confidence by tackling new challenges.

Create and keep a journal. List impressions, draw verbal pictures of people you meet and observe, even create a poem. You'll value it later.

Cash Conscious?

If you are on a budget, watch for seasonal savings on trips to Alaska. Holland America sometimes offers 50% off on its Denali cruise tours if you wait and watch their Web site. As this book was going to press, a cruise on Holland was listed at about $1,000 per person, interior cabins, but you still must manage your own transportation. (Google "Alaska on a Budget" to investigate bargains.)

If you are a savvy trip planner, you can put together a good visit at Alaska's magnificent national parks. A visit to Denali is worth saving for.

7

The Galapagos Islands

The land of giant tortoises, blue-footed boobies, and Darwin's finches would be my "natural selection" in late fall 2007. The Galapagos Islands is a *National Geographic* adventure, with you (and the giant tortoise) as the subject of the photo article.

To visit the Galapagos Islands, you must first fly into Ecuador. The eighteen islands of the Galapagos chain belong to Ecuador even though the Galapagos are six hundred miles out in the Pacific Ocean. Our small tour group flew into the capital city, Quito, and stayed in a hotel. The next day we flew east over the mountains into the Amazon basin. The sixteen travelers, plus our guide Roberto, transferred to a power boat, then motored up the Napo River for thirty-five miles, gaping at the dense jungle on both sides of the river. Upon landing at the jungle lodge, we were introduced to three days of jungle exploration. Surprisingly, Yachana Lodge was owned by a native Kentuckian who now claimed the Amazon jungle as his home. He had also established schools for the local children and provided employment for their parents.

Before venturing into the jungle, we were issued tall rubber boots and instructed to wear them. At night, we would leave the boots outside our cabin door. The tour director said, "In the morning tip them over and shake vigorously to get rid of spiders or other unfriendly critters." Roberto was a native Galapagoian, born in the islands. Only a true native can actually establish a home in this island chain. Even the number of visitors is restricted, so I felt honored that I would be able to visit the territory of Darwin's explorations.

Roberto was also knowledgeable about the jungle and guided us in the first part of our trip in Ecuador. He pointed out the wildlife in the tropical rain forest—interesting since I had recently visited the temperate rain forest in Alaska. At one point a colorful toucan took a liking to one man's hat and sat on his head as we trekked through the jungle. Roberto pointed out the different trees in the jungle that the natives use for medicine. He remarked that several U.S. pharmaceutical companies were interested in learning about the trees. Occasionally we would come across a little house in the jungle with a small garden, chickens clucking and running around in the yards. Talk about free-range chickens! It truly reminded us of farms in the U.S. Chickens are chickens and look and smell the same.

Deep in the jungle we met a medicine man who attempted to teach us how to use a blowgun. Rule number one: Don't inhale! Though featured in B movies from the '40s and '50s as lethal weapons wielded by glowering natives hidden in the trees to get rid of the white man, the guns are now used only for hunting. A few of us went tubing on the piranha-infested (as we later learned) Napo River, ate a roasted beetle (crunchy but tasty), and enjoyed the night sky. Electricity was available only between the hours of 6 p.m. and 10 p.m. But the pitch darkness of the nights allowed us to enjoy the sky on our night hikes. The stars were absolutely luminous, and the southern hemisphere's constellations are different than the ones in our northern hemisphere.

We weren't back in Quito very long before we boarded another plane and started to fly to the Galapagos Islands, with one small glitch. Our plane developed engine trouble halfway across the ocean. We returned to Ecuador to board another plane. I have learned while traveling to sit back and enjoy the ride, not allowing myself to get upset by unforeseen happenings, be it engine failure, lost luggage, or the grumpiness of one of your fellow travelers who takes a dislike to you.

We finally landed safely in the small airport on the island of Santa Cruz in the Galapagos. The first stop on land was to meet the giant tortoises that lumber along at an incredibly slow speed. Perhaps their slow rate helps them live to be 150 years old. Another lesson learned: slow down.

About sunset, we boarded a 135-foot luxury ship, with shiny wooden floors and gleaming brass rails. However, this luxurious ambiance did not help the seasickness that took hold of me as soon as we set sail. I was the only traveler who spent the first few hours embracing the porcelain toilet in my cabin! The others were solicitous and offered all kinds of remedies for seasickness. But I knew from experience this too would pass.

From this beautiful ship we explored the other islands and enjoyed the native habitat and animals—a page from *The Origin of Species*: albatross (well known from "The Rime of the Ancient Mariner"), iguanas, ospreys, enough red crabs to turn the rocks into colorful streams, and seals! Seals were everywhere, even lying on the wooden benches. Rules are strictly enforced on the islands: stay on the pathways, do not touch the wildlife, and absolutely no littering.

I was introduced to snorkeling one sunny day. I struggled into a wet suit (another first) and was instructed to clench the snorkel's mouthpiece between my teeth and fall into the water. A couple of sea lion pups suddenly joined me in the water, cavorting and swimming alongside. When one of the plentiful pelicans landed close to my head, that was enough for the big papa sea lion to come lumbering off the sandy beach and corral the pups to another area.

My first trip to South America was memorable also for meeting a roommate from Michigan for the first time. She had recently lost her husband who, she said, had always wanted to visit the Galapagos. She was enjoying the trip for two. We decided to try to travel together at some point in the future, though we have not yet done that.

Some things seemed universal in the places we saw, particularly for women. There always seem to be meals to prepare, floors to be swept, children to be cared for. It was touching to see mothers who lived in the jungle, along the Napo River, washing clothes in the river, chatting with other women, just living every day like women all over the world. They beat and scrubbed the clothes on the rocks. How they got those shirts that white in that river was a puzzle to me. It would make an interesting commercial for Tide, which they were using.

One morning I got up early and was invited to ride along on the school boat (canoe) that is used as a school bus. The schoolchildren, backpacks slung over their shoulders, always wait along the river bank to be rowed off to school in the nearby village, just as they could have been standing on any small town street in the U.S. waiting for a bus. Their shirts were sparkling white, as were their tennis shoes. What pride their mothers must have felt in being able to get those children off to school with white shirts and shoes pounded on those rocks.

Tips:

From the magic Cs, highlight openness to change: Don't be afraid of new experiences. Welcome them! Leave your old prejudices and stereotypical views of people behind. A witch doctor may really have something to teach you, even if it isn't how to cure your cold with armadillo poop pills.

You can cultivate the habit of adventuring with food. I don't recommend going overboard: huge portions of completely unfamiliar things may upset your system. I enjoyed one fried insect, but a plateful would not have been welcome Try a bite or two of something you wouldn't have ever thought of eating, and you may be surprised and like it! Americans have the reputation of scorning anything but cheeseburgers, so it's also good manners to try native food.

8

Destination: Morocco

Morocco: Casablanca, the bazaars, the Casbah, a trip to North Africa. After our plane landed, our first stop was Rick's Café for a quick photo shoot. The sound of Dewey Wilson quietly singing and playing "As Time Goes By" was circling in my head, along with the jet lag, in November 2008. At age eleven, I had stared up at the movie screen knowing Bogie was talking to me when he uttered the line, "We'll always have Paris." I strolled out of the theatre starry-eyed over Bogie's attention. And here I was in Casablanca. No Bogie, no Dewey, but entrancing anyway.

During World War II, Casablanca had been a meeting place for Roosevelt and Churchill along with the leading generals and navy admirals. Later, Churchill proclaimed Casablanca as one of his favorite cities and actually maintained a home there that overlooked the Atlantic Ocean.

Morocco is a small country, ruled by a young king who has attempted to modernize the country. He has installed electricity in the outlying areas, and the new paved roads are incredible. We traveled around the country in a large bus, passing pastures with sheep galore. The guide told an amusing story about President and Mrs. Clinton. It seems they enjoy Morocco, too, and Mrs. Clinton on one visit wanted to walk alone in one of the many pastures. Unbeknownst to her, the "shepherds" in the fields tending their sheep were actually security men dressed as shepherds. Is that true or a tourist guide fabrication? Who knows.

We traveled into the Sahara Desert, where we had an opportunity to take a camel ride—not to be sneered at. The camels themselves, though, seemed to sneer and slobber a lot. Dare I say, the camels do not offer the most comfortable rides, even with the pillows offered by the camel jockeys. I was sore for a week.

We then drove further and further into the desert, by this time riding in SUVs, speeding through the sand and dust to a three-day stay at a tented camp. Some of us liked to stroll among the sand dunes, but we were warned not to get too close to the country next door, Algeria. And where was the boundary line? I asked. Obviously, no "Welcome to Algeria" signs were stuck in the sand. They weren't specific.

One night I slept through a sandstorm and didn't even know it. I woke up out there in the desert, with everything in the tent covered with sand, including my bed.

During that tent stay in the desert, we were fortunate enough to be introduced to a nomad family who lived a wandering life with their goats and camels close by outside their tents. Three generations lived in the tent and moved from one place to another. I later worried that their way of life, which seemed normal and satisfying to them, would come under extreme pressure with the modernization and electrification of the country. I wished I could live with them and document their living arrangements for future generations to be aware of before it was obliterated.

We moved on to Marrakesh, a modern, metropolitan city. One early morning, some of us were able to take a balloon ride across the city. Once airborne, we could enjoy the city from afar.

I was sitting in an outside restaurant one day enjoying the atmosphere, with all sorts of people flying by on motorbikes—men and women dressed in business suits or their native Muslim dress complete with colorful hijabs. My adventurous spirit flared, and I wanted to have my picture taken on a motorbike. I looked across the street, and lo and behold, there was a bike rental establishment with several motorbikes parked out in front. I walked over and the owner came running out of his little house. I didn't speak his language and he didn't speak mine. The Moroccan people speak three languages: French, Arabic, and Berber, and I scored zero on all of these. I held up my camera and attempted to ask if he would take my picture on the black bike parked nearby. He shook his head and loudly proclaimed, "No, no!" Disappointment. He then pointed to a shiny red bike and nodded his head. Oh! He wanted his best bike photographed. I like to share the photo of me on the red bike and regale people about my tooling around Marrakesh. You don't actually have to do an activity in a foreign land to feel like you have experienced it.

I learned if you are pleasant, even though you can't speak the language, a smile gets you a long way. I was determined to learn another language when I got home—a goal I am still working on.

Tips:

Pleasantness and patience, always excellent qualities in living, can help dissolve language barriers. Good humor goes a long way in a foreign land. But definitely see if you can brush up on a language you took in school or sign up for a course in a foreign language. Even a few words help you get around more smoothly than if you are a complete non-speaker. And using the local language delights shopkeepers and café waiters and may get you a bargain or the best table.

Sitting and watching the people go by in any foreign land is a great education and off-the-beaten-track experience. Seek out those off of the main tourist paths, but be careful: exploring alone in most countries isn't safe. Sitting at a café and watching life go by is.

Curiosity, one of our Cs to expand your life, can also help you get beyond the tourist-trap experience. Befriend your guide; try to be courteous and prompt in standing up front when the group assembles or reassembles. You can ask questions about everyday life in the spot you are visiting and find out little-known facts and interesting stories. Whether you are in Morocco or touring the James Whitcomb Riley Museum Home in Indianapolis with a group, you will find the tour guide can share his/her personal knowledge about family life, dining customs, and the quirks and odd habits of the people who lived there. The guide will generally be glad to share or perhaps show off his/her accumulated knowledge.

However, take tourist guide stories with a grain of salt. Many may be apocryphal, exaggerated, or fourteenth-hand. I do think their agencies work with them to have accurate sources, but people will be people. Still, it is entertaining to encourage them to talk.

Beware of politics as a subject in a given country. If you have the rare privilege of getting inside a private home, as I did on some group tours abroad, you can carefully explore the issues of that country, but be sure not to express too many of your own opinions, particularly in a strong way. Our parents' advice to avoid the subjects of religion and politics in company is especially good caution when traveling.

Cash Conscious?

If you travel abroad, visit your local bank before you leave the U.S. You may get a better rate of currency exchange.

If you are going far across the world and you will be in a place with new foods, strange language, and some hint of danger from time to time, it's best not to plan a budget adventure. Stick with a group or go somewhere manageable and local to agree with your budget.

Speaking of that, how about an adventure near Halloween at the stately and impressive Hannah House on the south side of Indianapolis? It's said to be one of the ten best "authentically" haunted houses in America. It's free at certain times of the year. The Indiana Medical History Museum is the last historic building still standing on the grounds of "Seven Steeples," or the old Central Indiana Hospital for the Insane on Vermont Street in Indianapolis. It's spooky enough in the daytime; at night this 1896 building with its original experimental autopsy equipment is a real adventure. Or drive through Crown Hill Cemetery to James Whitcomb Riley's tomb—or ask at the cemetery office for a tour of the trees of the cemetery, a huge variety.

Enough of Adventures with the Dead! On an historical note, in Vincennes be sure to take in William Henry Harrison's house Grouseland and the Territorial Capitol for a mild but interesting adventure. Not everything that's exciting new fun has to be expensive.

9

Destination: Australia

If I were younger, I would move to Australia for at least a year. Why? Because it has so much to offer and the Australians love to recreate—they are on the move constantly. These are people on the cutting edge of adventuring. Sydney has five million people, and one in five owns a boat! With its sparkling water and blue skies, Sydney Harbor is an open invitation to get the sails up or turn on the motor and get out on the water.

The only drawback to Australia is that it's halfway around the world. It took us 15.5 long, boring hours to fly nonstop from California to Melbourne, the second-largest city in Australia. These people define pushing out the edges of the box, and they do it big time. Take sports for instance. Our tour viewed a soccer arena that holds 156,000 people and also the huge and classy Rod Laver Arena, where the Australian tennis matches are held each year. But there are bustling towns all over the place; Australia is huge, and everywhere we went there was activity and physical sport. You just had to respond in kind and get going.

In Adelaide some of us swam in the Indian Ocean. In Alice Springs we were introduced to the Aborigines, the native people of the continent. The Aborigine mothers, we learned, do not discipline their children; that is the duty of the aunts. The children only go to school until they are fifteen. If you want to take home a photographic memory, you'll be disappointed, as we were. Visitors to the country and local residents also are not allowed to take pictures of the Aborigines; they cannot even be in the background of a photo.

Cultural customs are interesting. After the death of an Aborigine, no likeness of that person can be saved. If he or she had been frescoed on a wall, that person's face must be whitened out, as we saw at a local school. In earlier years, these original inhabitants of Australia placed their dead in the trunks of big mahogany trees so the souls lived on in the tree. When the Europeans arrived and saw the bodies in the trees, they thought they were man-eating trees. Aborigines also have an interesting view of birthdays. They never say the celebrant is getting older; they say the celebrant is getting better! Incidentally, they do not care for white people. They think we smell bad, "like sour milk or rotten meat." We felt put in our place, and that isn't all bad for a race that is viewed as always arrogant.

Alice Springs is in the outback, hot, dry, and filled with flies. It is the stopping point to Ayres Rock—the huge iconic symbol of the country, six miles around the base. The mystery remains: how did such a huge rock end up in the middle of Australia? The Ayres Rock has recently been returned to the Aborigines, and they have given this religious and geographic landmark its original name, Uluru. It had been and is now a sacred place for them and the largest monolith in the world.

The Aussies love to eat. We saw many outdoor restaurants in the cities with people laughing and enjoying life with each other. I was introduced to kangaroo meat at a barbeque. Some even like to eat it raw. I prefer not to eat it at all. This is adventure carried too far, especially since I had just seen cute little kangaroos hopping around the day before at the park. Thankfully there also was shrimp and lobster to enjoy.

At Port Douglas on the northeast coast, we took a boat to a small island on the Great Barrier Reef, where we snorkeled and viewed the multicolored but fragile coral. While snorkeling in the clear water, I saw a big green leatherback turtle swimming under me. It was a beautiful sun-filled day on the coast of Australia.

From there we ventured farther north to Cape Tribulation. In this island area in the middle of a tropical forest, with no electricity except for generators, and crocodiles around us, our coastal hotel was a magical place. If one wanted to run away to the South Sea island of Dorothy Lamour and Bob Hope movies, this would be the island. I was introduced to tree surfing (also known as zip lining). I chose a helmet marked "Indiana Jones." We had to walk up what seemed like a thousand steps to get to the top of the tropical forest and look out over the Coral Sea. We were to be attached with wire rigging to a sliding hitch that would let us soar over the treetops.

The blokes running the activity looked at me, the only American, and seemed to want to say something. What would it be? I wondered. "Because of your country, our country remained free during World War II," this cool-looking attendant explained. I was touched. The first major naval battle won by the U.S. Navy was set on the Coral Sea. Australia would have been occupied by the Japanese if their attack there had been successful.

Every time it was my turn to zip down the line to the next platform in the trees, the attendants would sing the theme song to the movie Indiana Jones.

At Cape Tribulation, I gained a new friend from Montana, who had been chosen senior athlete of the state. We kayaked in the Coral Sea, as sunset painted the clouds and the mist rose, enveloping the mountains to the west and making the experience that much more exhilarating.

Seeing the famous Opera House in Sidney put a final stamp on our visit, the end of a wonderful trip to Australia. When you fly to Australia from Los Angeles, you lose a day. Consequently, when you return, you gain a day. Time and tide wait for no man, except when you are flying to the U.S. from Australia

Tips:

Realistically assess your ability to travel on long trips. The bus is going to northern or southern Indiana from your town, and its destination is at the other end of the state? Will you be uncomfortable or otherwise inconvenienced or harmed by sitting several hours? Australia is a long way, but so is Asia and really anywhere overseas. Ask the right comfort and health questions as you sign up for a trip. Medications easy to take? Exercise necessary for some reason for you? Climate acceptable for your situation or preference?

What kind of liability is involved in your adventuring on a trip? If you go snorkeling, who holds the insurance risk? Who holds the responsibility if you go up in a balloon and it bumps to the ground, injuring you? What is the reputation of the travel group? Online critiques and blogs are plentiful, and you can learn a lot about the quality and quirks of a given travel agency or tour, but remember people show off online, and asking a friend of acquaintance who has traveled with the tour is probably your best bet. Most of all, don't let someone's negative opinion of a country talk you out of a trip. Some people just like to gripe, and the Internet gives them a huge arena in which to do it.

The word "weird" doesn't apply to experimenting when you are travel adventuring. I got pretty good at throwing a boomerang.

Cash Conscious?

Do an Internet search for "Budget Trips to Australia." You will need to think about whether transportation costs are included in the trip package. As always, *caveat emptor*. Let the buyer beware.

10

Destination Europe: Ireland, Paris, Spain

You'll remember that I had made a list, preparing for adventuring while I was still caretaking. "Travel as much as is feasible" was near the top of the list. Then, in the last days of my work life at the state library, I set a specific goal: Visit all the continents of the world. Ireland seemed the perfect country to visit to fulfill the European stop on my continent list in November 2009. As a librarian, I thought it a good idea to visit the land of so many well-known authors: James Joyce, Oscar Wilde, W. B. Yeats, Samuel Beckett, and G. B. Shaw, to name a few. Half of my forbears emigrated from Kerry County, Ireland: the Foleys, the O'Learys, and the Phelans. (Guess I will get Germany on another trip.) For now, I wanted to experience shamrocks, rainbows, and Irish pubs. Everybody does. But I also wanted to do whatever else might come up as serendipity. Serendipity is usually more fun than the predictable travel stops. We landed in Shannon on the western coast of Ireland and toured the southern part of the country.

Ireland is full of castles and churches, and I think we visited all of them. The weather, true to predictions, was rainy but provided lots of green fields and lovely rainbows. I was intrigued by the stone fences, constructed in the eighteenth or nineteenth centuries and still standing and in use. We stopped at Blarney Castle and did the touristy thing: kissed the Blarney Stone. I had always envisioned the Blarney Stone as this big stone out in the middle of a green field that everyone trooped over rolling, sheep-clad hills to visit, and yes, kiss. I was surprised to find the stone on the roof of Blarney Castle. You access it by climbing hundreds of steps up a dark, narrow, curving cobblestone stairway. And in order to get the luck offered by kissing the stone, you have to lie down on your back, lean your head down this square hole and, if you could leave your head in there long enough not to get dizzy, you might be able to actually see the Blarney Stone. I, for one, had my head in the hole long enough for a quick thrown kiss, and I was up and out.

My roommate, originally from Georgia, liked a nip of Jack Daniels every afternoon. So when we visited an Irish pub, The Rag, to listen to the local music, it wasn't hard to convince her to ditch the music and move right into the bar area. The Rag could have been a scene in the TV series *Cheers*. The regulars were sitting around the bar at 4 p.m. on what seemed to be their accustomed stools. With camera in hand, I timidly asked Ritchie, a friendly red-faced Irishman, if I could take his picture. He was more than willing, grabbed me around the waist, and started whispering sweet nothings in my ear. By the time we left the bar, all the other regulars had more than agreed to be in our pictures.

We had had the travel stops; Richie and his raucous bar-sitters were the serendipity, one of the highlights of my trip to Ireland. I'll bet my female Irish ancestors would agree.

When I received a card from my usual travel agency explaining a river cruise in Paris at Christmastime was being offered at a reasonable cost, I had to sign up. "Christmas on the Seine" would be an unexpected surprise. It also surprised me that it was so cheap and that I could make up my mind within three weeks of liftoff from JFK in New York. I have gotten so I can pack in two hours. And so, deciding to miss for once the traditional family Christmas celebrations, I took the opportunity. Paris was all I had imagined: the Louvre, the Palace of Versailles, the Musée de Montmartre, the Arc de Triomphe, and the marvelous Eiffel Tower that was resplendent at night covered with white twinkling lights. Our riverboat, *M.S. Bizet*, was docked on the West Bank of the Seine. I love to throw "the West Bank" into a conversation to impress people. How French can you get? Since I was a last-minute passenger, I wasn't even listed on the passenger list.

I was assigned a room with a woman from Arizona (originally from Brooklyn). One problem: She thought she had a single room and was quite surprised (and a little miffed) when she came into the small shipboard compartment and found me passed out in the other twin bed. We had some bumpy moments, but after a few conversations, we ironed out our differences and became quite good friends.

She and I stood in line at the Eiffel Tower for over an hour. December in France is not a good time to be standing outside. After being whisked to the top of the tower overlooking the city of Paris, we knew the wait was well worth it. On our way back to our ship, we took the Metro and had to ask for help to get on the right train. Don't believe what you hear about the unfriendly French people; they were very helpful.

I do not care for cruises with thousands of people, but found that a river cruise (one hundred people) can be quite familial. The food offered by the French chef at every meal was excellent. The French love their food and enjoy each course—sometimes six. An evening meal can last over two hours, sometimes three, but with good newfound friends, it can be a memorable time.

Since my grandson was studying in Barcelona for a spring semester, my daughter and I had a good reason to visit him in Spain. This trip was on our own, without aid from a travel company. Our hotel was a block from the beach. The whole city of Barcelona was transformed when the Olympics was held there in 1992. Barcelona is noted for its architecture, churches, and museums. The Sagrada Família is a monumental cathedral initiated by the famous Spanish architect Antoni Gaudí. It is still being worked on more than one hundred years after building first began. Reputedly, Gaudí knew it would not be completed in his lifetime but said, "My boss [God] is in no hurry. He has all the time in the world." The cathedral draws thousands of tourists each year who admire Gaudí's vision of Christ's birth, crucifixion, and ascension.

Barcelona was the home of many artists. Picasso proclaimed it one of his favorite cities. I rode on a bus tour around the city and learned much about its history. My grandson introduced us to the Metro and the Spanish family with whom he was living. Luckily, he was fluent in Spanish.

Barcelona is located on the Mediterranean Sea. The harbor is filled with ships, both commercial and private. The sandy beach area is spectacular. Because our hotel was close to the beach, I spent many mornings strolling along the sandy shore, dipping my feet in the cold Mediterranean. Many native Barcelonans visit and enjoy the beaches. (I'll save the experience of my foray into nude beach country for a later story.)

We commented on the fact that the Spanish people in that area were not too friendly. Smiles were not returned, and they seemed rather dismissive at times. However, while walking back from the beach one day, I got lost—totally turned around. I had a notepad from our hotel, good thinking, so when I asked for directions, I held up the hotel name. Of the six people I asked, only two could speak English, and I had no recognizable Spanish. All of the six I asked were helpful and friendly, though, and went out of their way to help me locate my hotel. Maybe one has to be in need before the true Spanish hospitality emerges. Another challenge while traveling: getting lost. It can be scary but a great learning experience.

Tips:
Make up your mind that if you can't get the ideal roommate, you will try to survive with the one you have. "If you can't be with the one you love, love the one you're with." You have had enough of life to adjust to almost anyone, and trying to do that can enlarge your perspectives (and patience). Still, if it's unbearable, there's always a request to the tour director for a switch.

Don't automatically assume people are unfriendly because they don't understand your language. Try several people before you give up, and you're pretty sure to find someone to help you when you need it. And take a pad and pencil and native language dictionary with you. Written words are easier to decipher than our poorly pronounced foreign terms.

    Philosophically, I'll say this to you about our allotted hours of life:
- o Do not let time deter you or hold you back.
- o Arrange necessary tasks in order to leave time to do everything in life you want to do. Time is a commodity in itself.
- o Be creative with your time, but treat it with reverence. It is measured out to us.

11

Destination: Egypt

No obvious signs of a revolt appeared when I entered Egypt in August 2010; however, tourists seemed to be very well protected. We had armed guards on our buses when we traveled around the country. A machine gun was mounted to the back of the riverboat we boarded in Luxor to sail down the Nile. It wasn't that obvious, but I discovered the gun when I became curious and decided to inspect the boat. While I was walking around the pyramids, I bumped into a security guard (they were easy to spot as they were the only ones in suits in the 100-degree weather) and noticed he had an Uzi under his jacket. Oops! They did well to protect their tourists because tourism has always been a major source of income for the country. I will say at no time did I feel threatened, and I walked alone on the streets every chance I could in downtown Cairo.

Our guide, Amin, represented Egypt well. He was truly in love with his country and was so knowledgeable about all aspects, present and past. In traveling abroad, most guides I have met have been well versed, but Amin was exceptional. He remarked one day, "I had to attend classes for two years before I was accepted as a tour guide." Amin guided us to every tomb and sculpture in the country with vast amounts of knowledge, enhanced with good humor.

We visited the Egyptian Museum in Cairo to get a feel of what we would be introduced to in this intriguing country. The museum itself was just as you would imagine in Egypt or had seen in the movies: stone floors, light streaming through the high windows, dust particles filtering through the rays, and hundreds of Egyptian artifacts, including a copy of the Rosetta Stone, King Tut's many gold-plated coffins, chariots and wooden boats used as hearses, an embalming table similar to our modern ones, huge stone statues of Egyptian kings, and so much more.

While in Cairo, we visited the pyramids of Giza. They are the most famous ancient monument in the world. Although they look smooth from a distance, the pyramids were constructed using large irregular stone blocks and so are rough and uneven at close range. When new, they would have gleamed brilliant white in the sunlight. With camera in hand, a true Kodak moment, I rode a camel around the pyramids and found that the camels in Egypt are not any friendlier or more comfy than the ones in Morocco. They all like to drool and spit and are generally disagreeable. But they are wonderfully built animals. They are not called Ships of the Desert for nothing.

The Sphinx is truly a mysterious marvel from the days of ancient Egypt. The body of a lion with the head of a king or god has come to symbolize strength and wisdom. It was commissioned during the fourth dynasty, in 2558 BC, by Khafra, one of the sons of Cheops, who is recognized as the builder of the Great Pyramid. The paws of the Sphinx are fifty feet long and fourteen feet wide.

We flew to Luxor, then after viewing the Aswan High Dam and Lake Nasser (filled with crocodiles), we traveled south by bus to explore the incredible temples of Abu Simbel. They were carved into solid rock three thousand years ago, but almost as impressively, in 1960, in a monumental feat of modern engineering, these massive temples were moved to their present location when construction of the Aswan High Dam created Lake Nasser and flooded their original location. It is incredible that we can still enjoy statues thousands of years old in the twenty-first century.

Early one morning we took a hot-air balloon ride over the Valley of the Kings after exploring its sandy caverns the day before. While you are floating above the Nile River, you see the contrast between the Nile's green floodplain and the surrounding desert. The waters of the Nile River have been Egypt's lifeblood since ancient times. Crops in the fertile delta of the Nile depended on the seasonal flooding in the past and rely on irrigation from the Nile today.

After flying back to Cairo, we boarded a train to Alexandria at a very busy train station. As a librarian I was thrilled to be able to visit the modern descendent of the oldest library in the world, built in 332 BC by Alexander the Great. The Bibliotheca Alexandrina, Egypt's leading cultural institution, was built to honor the past, to celebrate the present, and to invent the future. The library has been completely modernized with triangular skylights, modern movable bookshelves, and banks of computers. The library is still impressive because of its history and the tradition of the original library of Alexandria. It is located close to the Mediterranean Sea. Before reboarding the train to Cairo, we convinced our guide to let some of us have a dip in the Mediterranean. I would later revisit the Mediterranean Sea in Spain.

I enjoyed visiting Egypt and hope our great guide, Amin, and his family are safe and well with the unrest in the country at the time of this writing. Egypt has so much to offer: the antiquities, the friendly people, and the opportunity for us to revel in its lengthy history. It is a shame to cross this country off your travel list. I feel so fortunate to have visited the ancient home of the Nile.

If you have any sense of history and its importance to our lives, you will enjoy exploring Egypt. The amazing engineering feats of building the tombs and statues, accomplished in the years before modern machinery, is truly astonishing.

Tips:
If in your travels you elect to go up in a hot-air balloon, you will be going up in the early morning just after sunup or in the evening just before sundown. That's when balloons can travel best. You'll be stepping up high to get into the balloon and, obviously, it will be a challenge for someone who fears heights. For me, the view and thrill were worth all of that. One of the most interesting balloon rides in our state is the 1859 balloon voyage at Conner Prairie, mentioned earlier in the tips on volunteering. Though it is tethered, there is a tremendous thrill as the balloon goes up, higher and higher, 350 feet above Hamilton County, then after you have savored the spectacle of small trees like bushes and toy-like people, back down again.

With this ride, you can experience some of the "high" thrill of ballooning while still tied to the ground.

I learned from the Egypt trip that we must use every day as an opportunity for growth and appreciation of the travel available to us. People fear to travel to Israel and other middle eastern nations because of possible danger, but millions are still going safely. These nations provide security; their economies depend on it. Don't let fear of the unknown hold you back unnecessarily, just investigate security issues thoroughly. Your tour or travel agent may supply information about security, but I wouldn't depend on them alone. There are important points to be weighed. The U.S. Department of State issues travel warnings about countries where unrest or danger for citizens may occur. As of March 29, 2012, for instance, when this piece about Egypt was being prepared, the State Department warned citizens "to remain alert to local security developments and be vigilant regarding their own personal security." You can check Travel.State.Gov, a service of the Bureau of Consular Affairs.

My advice is to avoid Egypt, or any other destination, when such a warning is in place. But barring that, don't alter your travel plans out of non-specific, rumor-fed fear. That kind of vague fear can stop us all from ever going anywhere in our day and age. One never knows what's going to happen in the future, sometimes the near future, so enjoy the here and now and set your travel plans in motion.

Tipping is expected, and you need to have that process fully explained for the particular place you will be visiting in advance. Do you know the origin of the word "tip"? It is said that in the coffeehouses of the seventeenth century in London, where many classes of society gathered to chat and drink chocolate and coffee, waiters could be urged to bring a certain table's coffee before serving other customers if money was passed to the waiter with a note: T.I.P. It meant "to insure punctuality." On my first overseas trip, tipping was not clearly explained. So when our guide suggested "4-6 dollars a day" I understood her to say "$46 per day." Needless to say when my tour guide opened my tip envelope, she was more than a little surprised. I didn't tell my kids. If they knew my generosity (or klutziness), they wouldn't let me out of my own zip code.

Value the excellent tour guide and tip him or her accordingly. The percentage depends on the number of days and the intensity of work the guide has undertaken for your group. It is usually noted in your pre-travel plans.

At the beginning of this section on traveling, I mentioned the obvious: it's not always possible or easy for everybody to travel to faraway exotic places. I suggested going to a nearby small town to get a burger and visit the local museum. This is a very satisfying adventure—if the burgers are good and the museum is still open. Be aware that local museums in many states including Indiana have closed in recent years for financial reasons. Some still open and interesting to visit are the Indiana Military Museum in Vincennes, the Ernie Pyle Home in Dana, the Indiana Railways Museum in French Lick, and the Auburn Cord Duesenberg Museum in Auburn. You can check local museums on the web site of the Association of Indiana Museums (http://www.indianamuseums.org/). And as for the best burger, stop any local resident on the street. They always know. Or make it a salad for fitness's sake!

China (2006) was a true "photo op" location. A tranquil Tiananmen Square in the heart of Beijing brought many visitors armed with only cameras. All the photo bugs are thrilled with the historic sites in China. I had to buy a one-time-use camera to capture my memories.

Australia, 2009. It looks like I am letting my friend from Montana do all the paddling while kayaking on the Coral Sea in Australia. The waters were rough at sundown, so I did my share of paddling as we rounded the curve of the island and encountered wild waves.

Morocco (2008) The lack of modern conveniences adds to the thrill of tenting in the Sahara Desert in sand land. Our outhouse lacks some frills but "running water" awaited us in the old teakettle seen here on the conveniently located chair for hand washing. All of these photos are from my collection.

In Morocco it was eye-opening to meet a nomad family of three generations living in the Sahara Desert. Their large tent provided lots of room for all their possessions and was easily moveable for the next destination in the barren sands. Their camels and goats were close at hand and seemed totally uninterested in us.

Ecuador (2007) I was invited to ride along in an early morning school boat on the Napo River in the Amazon jungle in Ecuador. The kids stand patiently along the river in gleaming white shirts, tennis shoes, and knapsacks thrown over their shoulders, waiting to be picked up and rowed to the local school. They are shown here on their way there.

Spain (2012) The "bare essentials" of language skills would have helped me avoid the nude beach as I was walking along the Mediterranean in Barcelona, Spain, while humming "All of me."

Egypt (2010) A shipboard party as we floated on the Nile River in Egypt called for a new party dress, and I found it in the ship's small gift shop. The fringed headwear was sold on the street for one dollar.

Ireland (2009) I was meeting and making new friends in an Irish bar named The Rag. The Irish people, like many of my maternal ancestors, love to reach out and welcome you into their afternoon get-togethers.

Richie and I became Best Friends for Five Minutes in the bar in Ireland.

Section III
Adventuring Beyond the Boundaries

12

Learning To Kayak

Adventure for adventure's sake. It's a way of life, or at least of thinking. There is excitement in each day when we are able to open our thoughts to new life experiences. You don't have to wait for official retirement to begin welcoming adventure. While I was at the state library, I signed on for a "Woman's Adventure Weekend" held at a former Girl Scout camp south of Indianapolis. We were introduced to many outdoor activities, such as fly fishing, repelling, archery, canoeing, and kayaking. The minute I nestled into the seat of a kayak and the paddle stroked the water, I was hooked. I knew this was something I would enjoy and pursue. When I got out of the water, a group of women who were watching me asked, "Have you kayaked before? You look as though you belonged there." That did it!

I made arrangements to take kayaking lessons at the Indianapolis Natatorium on the grounds of Indiana University–Purdue University Indianapolis (IUPUI), close to home for this foray into a new experience. The fact is that every time you attempt or learn something new, you are adventuring, especially if you experience it alone.

I had never even been in the pool at the Natatorium, a huge swimming center where college swim meets and other major national water events are held. Going in by myself to take kayaking lessons was rather scary, particularly at age sixty-five! "What am I doing? Should I go in and take the kayaking lessons or not?" Fear raises its ugly head, undermining your sense of adventure. And who cares what others think, particularly at age sixty-five!

The lessons were taught by a man and wife who were expert kayakers. The wife was a mere slip of a thing with perfect make-up (waterproof, I assumed) and lustrous dark hair slicked back in

69

a ponytail. When she demonstrated the Alaskan Roll (rolling over and popping right back, introduced by Alaskan Indians), I was flabbergasted! That little lady could do that roll in a split second and bounce right back up, lipstick luminously red, not a hair out of place! Amazing!

After going over the rules of the water and completing several lessons in the kayaks in the water, I was assigned a young male instructor, who didn't seemed too thrilled to be drawing the "old lady" when there were several young girls in the class who looked pretty fetching in their swimsuits. He looked at me and proclaimed, "I'm going to teach you the Alaskan Roll." He didn't sound or look too positive about my kayaking abilities, but we pressed on. "Get in the kayak and strap yourself in. I'm going to turn you upside down and you stay underwater for twelve seconds. When you're ready to right yourself, just reach your arms up and tap on the bottom." After two and a half seconds, I was not only tapping on the bottom of the kayak, which was now on top, I was practically pounding. What I described later as my near-drowning event, he snidely called the fastest twelve seconds on record.

Lessons over, it was time for me to take my "skills" to the wild.

My first kayaking trip outside of Indiana was on the Colorado River with an Elderhostel group. Elderhostel, now named Road Scholar and mentioned elsewhere in this book, is a travel-and-learn association established for persons over the age of fifty and offers many affordable trips with reasonable housing around the country. The organization mostly offers lecture series, but "Active Trips" are also offered. Kayaking trips are definitely on the "active" page. The trips are labeled 1 through 5, with 5 being the most active, and each is described in terms of how much strength and stamina will be needed to keep up.

My kayaking group met in the old mining town of Chloride, Arizona, population four hundred. Our motel, facetiously called Shep's Bed & Breakfast, was something right out of the Old West and was owned by a man with a somewhat questionable past. Seems he'd had a high-powered position in the government, mostly in the Near East, before retiring and buying this old, out-of-the-way motel. What he lacked in hospitality, he made up for by hiring some wonderful cooks.

The copper mine in Chloride had closed many years ago, but there were some old timers left from the wild days. While walking around this literally one-horse town (it was an old white nag in a yard) I met an older woman taking an evening walk through the town, which consisted of one post office, a one-room library, and an old saloon that still sported the wooden bar. The woman, whom the motel owner later described to me as a "former lady of the night," gave me some history of Chloride when it was a roaring mining town. I also learned that the Chloride Post Office was the oldest continuously operating post office in Arizona.

The other fifteen kayakers on the trip (more experienced than I) were driving in from different areas of the West. I found that most of the people on the "Active List" were usually from the western states. Very few came from Indiana. We practiced kayaking on two small lakes in the vicinity. On the second day, one of our guides instructed us to row out to the middle of the lake, fall out of the overturned kayak, then upright the kayak and climb back in as quickly as we could. The guide wanted to be sure most of us could survive just in case. Luckily I had no trouble.

The next day, we took a van and all the kayaks to Hoover Dam, about twenty miles from Chloride. We put the boats in the water right below the dam (this was before 9/11 so the security was not so strict). When I first climbed in the kayak and started floating down the river, I looked around and could not believe how much natural beauty surrounded me. The river below the dam was so narrow I could see both sides of it, placid water meandering around and ahead at each bend of the river. Surrounding us were rock formations created eons before by the mighty Colorado River. It was truly awe-inspiring as well as immeasurably peaceful. Kayaking offers a different view of our country than what you see by car.

Kayaking is such a solitary sport. Even if you are with a group, you are really alone. There is an intoxicating solitude in paddling along below a beautiful blue sky with the tree-filled banks beside you. This is an activity that everyone should experience at least once in his or her life. The beauty of the outdoors is truly a blessing from above.

The interesting women I met on my first kayaking trip were also a blessing. One woman was the mother of a well-known author. She lived on a ranch in northern California; she was also a licensed pilot. She had been a pilot for Velma Johnston, a.k.a. Wild Horse Annie. Wild Horse Annie was well known in the West as a savior of the wild mustangs. Annie, a Nevada secretary, worked tirelessly to save the animals and was responsible for legislation that would help preserve the horses.

We pitched our tents and camped along the river at night. One morning we got up and headed for our makeshift breakfast area. A rattlesnake had discovered our food in the night and was now camped in our cereal. One of the guides captured the snake in a pillowcase. We took him down the Colorado River with us to the next camping area, where the previous campers had not been too tidy. Neatness is an unwritten law while camping in the wild. We dumped the snake in the rocks and hoped the messy campers would come back and be surprised by our rattler. Served them right.

We were on the river for five nights and finished our odyssey in Bullhead City. What a grand and glorious week it had been. I had made new friends, been introduced to the grand Colorado River, and survived my first kayaking trip.

Since that first kayaking trip, I have kayaked in many places: off the coast of Georgia near St. Simons Island; Sitka Sound in Alaska; rivers in Utah, Oregon, and Yellowstone National Park; and, as described earlier, in the Coral Sea in Australia. But my initial kayaking on the Colorado River remains in my memory like a beautiful photograph I can take out whenever I want to just by remembering.

Tips:

The Hoosier Canoe and Kayaking Club, established in 1963, offers exciting trips with others who want to canoe or Kayak to Indiana reservoirs lakes and rivers. More information can be found on the club's Web site at http://www.hoosiercanoeclub.org/. A variety of other organizations and clubs offer kayaking lessons.

Cash Conscious?
In the last couple of years kayaking has been made available inexpensively in Indiana's state parks. Brown County State Park and Lincoln State Park now have kayaking, and they are only two examples. Canoeing and launching your own boat is allowed at places such as Raccoon Lake State Recreation Area. Check with the state park sites or ask your library for information.

13

Stranded at the Train Station

I have never felt fear while kayaking on rivers, no matter how great the rapids. The rapids on the Rogue River in Oregon in 2003 were the most perilous, but I paddled through without upsetting, as some of the male kayakers did. The scariest time I experienced in these active kayaking days, however, was not in the water. It was after I got off the river and ended up standing alone on the platform of an abandoned railroad station in the middle of Utah.

I had flown into Salt Lake City and located the bus that would take me to the small town of Green River in the southeastern part of the state, which not surprisingly is situated on the Green River. I was supposed to meet the small group of kayakers at 5 p.m. The bus trip took longer than I had anticipated, and I was concerned about missing the 5 o'clock meeting. When we were a few miles south of Salt Lake City, the driver got a call on his phone and was told he had forgotten one of the passengers at the airport, so we had to turn around and go back and pick her up. Then the driver had to stop several times along the route to relieve himself. We did get there in time for the meeting, but thinking ahead, my return flight to Indiana was going to be hard to make, especially if I had the same driver with the weak bladder.

So when my week camping and kayaking along the Green River was finished, I decided to go back to Salt Lake City by Amtrak. Amtrak only stops in this small town if they are called and the conductor knows there is a passenger to pick up. I thought I was planning carefully, taking care to know the exact time of the train's arrival. I called the Amtrak number and was assured they would pull into the station "around 7:30 p.m." ("around" being the key word). I called the town's sole taxicab early, making sure not to miss the train, thoughts of that word "around" still in my head. While driving to the station, we passed a very lively, busy, cantina packed with patrons, some falling out the door already.

I arrived at 6:30 p.m., sun still high in the sky. To my surprise the train station was boarded up—completely abandoned. What had been at one time a bustling railroad connection was now dead. The taxi dropped me off and drove away, leaving me standing alone on an empty platform. My train was due in less than forty-five minutes; it would show up soon, wouldn't it? I waited and waited. It got darker and darker as I watched the sun sink slowly towards the western horizon. I had a cell phone; maybe I had better call someone. I was beginning to feel ET's plight—"phone home." Well, it seems the middle of Utah was not in my calling range. I had no luck reaching anyone, let alone home.

One huge overhead spotlight eventually came on. That was the only light in this dark, deserted station. As the only passenger waiting for the train, I didn't know if it was better to be in the light or in the dark, especially with the boys down the road getting louder and rowdier. Did I miss the darn train? I kept looking down the tracks. Where oh where was that train?

After several false noises I mistook for train whistles, finally at 8:30 p.m. I heard the train: a bright light down the tracks! I will never forget how relieved I was to see the flashing light of the train. I can still imagine it coming around the curve of the tracks. And it stopped, yes, praise be to Glory, it stopped! I was never so glad to see anything in my life. I ran up the steps, found an empty seat, and luxuriated in the safety of the Amtrak train—even though it was over an hour late.

Tips:
Don't trust the schedule Amtrak or any other transportation system gives you over the phone.

Carry cash—when I got on the train, the conductor insisted I pay in cash, which left me with one dollar to get back to Indiana. Since I seldom use my Visa card for cash, I couldn't remember my password. It was an interesting study in self-analysis when I sat in an airport and watched others stuff their faces with food while I had only one dollar to spend. If a person is hungry, she can become a little grumpy! I had missed my flight to Indiana; it was two in the morning, too late to get a motel, so I spent the rest of the night sitting in the Salt Lake City airport. I figured if I got robbed, the robbers wouldn't get much, just a dollar. So carry about $50 worth of cash when you travel.

Running for Public Office

If you want to go out on a limb for adventure, run for elected office in your hometown. I have experienced it twice, three times if you count a primary race. The first time I put my toe in the political waters was about 1994 in the northern Indiana town of Plymouth, where my husband and I reared our children. I ran as the Democratic candidate for city council because I thought no other woman had ever served on the council, and frankly, it was about time a female voice was heard.

I coerced a fellow worker with an artistic bent (a Republican, I found out later) into designing a business card positing my political credentials to pass out to all of my would-be constituents. The card displayed two pairs of legs in trousers and one pair of crossed legs (mine) in a dress under a conference table. Really cute! I won easily in the May primary and looked forward to the main election in the fall.

I found that as a politician I had to attend a lot of meetings, make speeches, march in parades, and smile a lot. Unfortunately, before my "breakout to adventure," I wasn't vocal enough in meetings and was not good at speeches. What was I going to speak about with no prior experience in the world of politics? However, I perfected my parade wave—almost like Queen Elizabeth II minus the big hat and handbag—into something to be admired. It's all in the elbow as you pass the crowds waiting to have candy tossed at them. And if you sometimes point at an important person along the parade route, it adds a certain pizzazz to the wave.

I ended up with too many cards, thanks to the printer who wouldn't print just fifty. As cute as they were, I still had to do something with five hundred cards, so I went door to door leaving behind one of my cards either with a person on in the mailbox. Honestly, running for an elected position is really hard work, especially if it is done right. I didn't do it right. The little effort I put into it still took a lot of time, and that made me admire the politicians who have the audacity and energy to do what it takes.

I lost in the fall election, but not by much, to a young man with prior experience in the political world. Then he decided after serving three years to give up the post and moved to a larger city. Oh, what might have been!

When I moved to the Indianapolis area, I lived in a predominantly Republican county. I found this out when I volunteered to work on the election board and was astonished to find that so many incumbents did not have any Democrat opponents. This didn't seem right to me. I decided I was going to run for office, and this time I might not fail. In the primary, I threw my hat in the ring of city council politics against another woman. I was still working at the Indiana State Library and had little time to campaign (rationalization: driving seventeen miles to work each way, plus getting a grandson to daycare every day). So what did I expect?

This lady beat me by six votes. The local newspaper tracked me down at the library and asked, "Are you going to ask for a recount?" I laughed and replied, "Absolutely not!"

Tips:
Everyone should get involved with politics in one way or another. It is a lot of work to run for office, so if you do run, take my advice and work behind the scenes before you announce your campaign so you have some idea of what goes into an election. Learn from my lessons. It is actually fun. You have not lived until you see a sign with your name in large block letters stuck in someone's front yard. Those yard signs are ego builders—until you have to take them down after your loss. I still have a few.

Filing procedures for public office vary with the office and jurisdiction. To run for the U.S. Senate and House of Representatives, you must file with the Federal Election Committee. For legislative representatives in the state House or Senate, governor, or other state offices, file with the Indiana Election Division, easy to access online and listed in your local telephone book. County and city office filing procedures can be found by calling the local authorities or visiting the county or city Web site.

Political parties also welcome your help. Visit the candidates' Web sites or campaign headquarters volunteer or be a paid worker. Step up and work at the polls at least once in your life.

Skiing

We've all heard the saying, "Sometimes the answer is no." My one-time experience with skiing in 2003 pushes the borders of adventuring for seniors. I tested the limits of my own desires and abilities and went into an area of risk. I now say, "Don't try any adventure that puts you at risk of physical harm or is too trying for a senior age level." I learned the hard way. The answer was "no" on this skiing thing.

Skiing looks so easy on TV. Just step into the boots, fasten them onto the skis, stand at the top of a hill, and with a little help from gravity, schuss down the hill. I had never tried skiing, so when I had a chance to visit Paoli Peaks, the Rocky Mountains of Indiana, I jumped at the chance. It isn't every day Paoli, Indiana, offers skiing. It's in southern Indiana. But they do make snow, and on one winter day, I decided to try this new sport.

After arriving at the Peaks, I went to the pro shop, which was packed with other skiers. I was fitted with the right size of ski boots, and I strapped on the skis given to me. "Lessons?" No, how hard could this be? I soon found out—even getting out the door wasn't easy. I was soon sliding along, working my way to the suggested easy Bunny Slope. Suddenly, I was moving, rapidly I might add, towards an orange plastic construction fence. After I bounced off the fence, my skis crossed in front of me, and I found getting up off this icy mess was something else I probably should have known about.

I finally got my skis straightened out and going in the direction of the hill. By this time Paoli Peaks was looking more like Pikes Peak. Struggling to the top of the little hill that was the Bunny Slope, I was beginning to wonder why I was here, when all of a sudden I found myself careening down that slope faster than I ever thought possible for one woman to go without benefit of a motor. Thank the good Lord above I missed hitting all the other skiers on the hill. As I swooshed past, I kept yelling, "Excuse me. Excuse me!" I didn't know if that was the proper etiquette, or if they could even hear me, traveling at the speed of sound as I was. I tried to apologize since I was flying down towards the end of the world and possibly my life.

I found my mode of stopping was falling over, suddenly. A nice young man, someone quite adroit on skis I might add, offered to help me up. He proceeded to give me a few tips on how to ski safely down the rest of the hill. The trouble was that by this time I was so traumatized, I was frozen, literally and figuratively, to the snow beneath me. I could not move. He finally convinced me to creep towards the bottom so I could crawl over to the tram to take me back to the ski-less world.

Who knew skiers sailed so fast down those snow-covered mountains? Obviously not me. Out of control is a frightening feeling; I never wanted it again. I had to get real. I could have injured someone seriously at that speed down the hill and surely myself, too. Breaking a bone (whether yours or someone else's) is not a good thing, and seniors are warned not to do so under any circumstances. I had been foolish.

I got back to the pro shop, unlatched everything on my feet, and was relieved to feel good solid terra firma beneath me. A grizzled pro shop employee came along and asked, "How did you like skiing for the first time?" After telling him about my near-death experience on the icy slopes, he said, "Didn't you take a lesson?" I muttered as I walked away, "Oh, shut up!" But he was right.

Tips:
Take a lesson (maybe two or three) before attempting to look like a Norwegian skier.

Really appreciate those skiers on TV. They have years of learning and discipline behind them.

Don't believe the sign that says "Bunny Slope. Degree of Difficulty: Easy."

If you just want to experience the ambiance by sitting before the fire and sipping hot chocolate in your cute knit hat and sweater, try the Indiana ski resorts: Perfect North Slopes in Lawrenceburg or the place of my doom, where others ski very happily, Paoli Peaks on State Road 25 outside of Paoli. Perfect North Slopes also offers "Mud-Stash" experiences in the summer. You would have to be an awfully adventurous senior to try sliding along through this obstacle course in the mud. Beyond my pay grade, as they say.

Cash Conscious?

It's a lot less expensive to stay right here in Indiana to ski and drive to the ski resort for the day than it is to journey out of state to Colorado or New England. Paoli Peaks offers discounts for military veterans and a teacher ski free day at certain times. Caberfae Peaks at Cadillac, Michigan, is a few hours' north of the Indiana line and during the most recent season had a $24 day-long pass for seniors. Ski equipment is available to rent.

16

Picture on a Nude Beach

As mentioned earlier in this book, on one trip I visited my grandson in Barcelona, Spain, that wonderful city with so many cultural activities and a statue of Christopher Columbus overlooking the harbor. After looking at the sights, I decided on something different. I'd see what the beach looked like.

Half a block from my hotel was the beach, an expansive sandy area sloping down to the beautiful blue Mediterranean Sea. The area often overflows with people walking, running, biking, and of course enjoying the sand, especially on the weekends in the spring, which is what this was. I was walking along the shore, splashing my feet in the cold Mediterranean, when looking down the shore line I saw a lot of bare butts. In fact, bare everything! I had strolled into the playa nudista or suitless shoreline. One part of the beach is set aside for those who wish to shed their clothing and frolic unencumbered by bathing suits. Some are sun worshippers. As for me, at my age I prefer keeping my clothes on. I don't care, though, if someone wants to take everything off to avoid tan lines.

However, as I was walking along the water, out of the corner of my eye I could see one of the no-tan-liners in full Monty walking towards me at a right angle. I knew at some point in the very near future we would intersect. What would I say? What is the proper way for a non-nudie to meet and greet a nudie? "Hello, nice seeing you?" Maybe not. Certainly not, "What's up?"

I picked up my pace, and we just missed each other. I walked further along and found a man sitting on the beach—fully clothed—and asked him to take my picture on this beach—quickly, if possible. So there you have this off-butt, I mean off-beat, adventure. Whenever anyone asks, "How was your trip to Spain?" I always answer, "I have pictures." Actually, they are disappointing, if you're wondering. Nobody's naked, especially not me.

>Tips:
>Watch the signs as you walk the beach.
>Don't judge people by what they are not wearing.

Mustangs

Many of us probably played Cowboys and Indians when we were little. I had a chance to be a real-life cowboy in May 2010, when I joined a group of women to observe wild mustangs in their native habitat in the Sierra Nevada Mountains in eastern California.

The word *mustang* comes from a Spanish word and means "stray livestock." These magnificent wild horses are feral descendants of sixteenth-century horses brought to North America by the Spanish. By the middle of the century, the Plains Indians, such as the Lakota, Crow, and Sioux, were capturing and taming them. Many mustangs are smaller than the average domesticated horse. Mustang herds organize themselves into a number of smaller bands, each headed by a stallion.

U.S. troops, including General George Armstrong Custer's Seventh Cavalry, also pressed them into service. It has been reported that the only survivor of the Battle of the Little Big Horn was a horse named Comanche, who was a mustang. At one time there were millions of wild horses, but now there are only about 37,000, and that number is not verifiable. In recent years the mustang population has been growing again, and roundups are held to relocate the horses from areas considered too crowded for them. I have always been interested in the mustangs and couldn't pass up an opportunity to see them.

When your destination is two thousand miles away, at an altitude of over seven thousand feet and out in the middle of nowhere, it is an adventure just getting there. I took a plane from Indy to Chicago, a plane from Chicago to San Francisco, and then a plane from San Francisco to Reno, Nevada. I had less than thirty minutes between each flight, so I was running through a lot of airports. When I landed in Reno and got my bag from the baggage return, I noticed it was rolling lopsided. The airline had knocked a wheel off my bag. I ran down the airline representative and complained about my bag. He said, "Oh, lady, we don't guarantee wheels. They're knocked off all the time." I gathered I wasn't going to win with him and figured I would take up my complaints again on my way back through Reno.

    I picked up rental car to drive 146 miles south to a little town called Benton Springs, California, where I was to meet the other members of the party. I noticed my rental car had no license plate. I could see what would happen if I were stopped by the state police on a strange road in a strange state with no license plate, and I went roaring back into the airport to offer another complaint.

    Leaving Nevada, I was finally on my way to Benton Springs. However, I unknowingly took a wrong turn and ended up on a beautiful pine tree-filled area circling a sparkling blue lake. I was driving around Lake Tahoe—nice, but not on my route. I pulled into a small commercial area to find out where I was. The lady said, "I bet you're lost," to which I quickly agreed. She got me back on the correct highway. Now all I had to do was drive another ninety miles on Rt. 395 and look for a turn-off road for the last forty-six miles east to Benton Springs.

    I finally came to the unmarked road. It was so desolate and deserted I met only two cars on the whole forty-six miles. The road was very hilly, just up and down, up and down. Apparently, this road had only been opened for two weeks; it is closed in the winter because of all the snow in this area. This part of eastern California is a well-known skiing area.

    I finally came to Benton Springs and found the motel—not difficult to find in a town of maybe five hundred people. The other participants in the horse-packing trip were there. There were eleven other women, and all but one was from the Golden State besides me. They were also horsewomen of the first caliber. Most had ranches and horses at home. They were a bit puzzled about a non-horsewoman from Indiana. More than one asked, "How did you hear about this trip?" I replied that I had read about it in the Phoenix paper once and saved it, thinking I would one day do it. Another question was, "You're from where?" I don't think they had ever met anyone from Indiana before, especially on a horse-packing trip.

These women were outdoorswomen and obviously had done a lot of camping. In addition, they were very interested in saving the wild mustangs from the Bureau of Land Management, which believes the mustangs have over-reproduced and need to be taken away from public lands. Part of the money for this trip went to saving the mustangs.

The next morning we left the motel and drove about ten miles up into the mountains. We were introduced to the horses with whom we would be spending time the next week. The largest horse was standing in front of me. I turned to the lady next to me and said, "I hope that's not my horse." It was. His name was Lite. Lite turned his head towards me, and as our eyes met, we knew immediately who was boss. He was. He would show me later on the mountain trails how he would let me know.

We packed up our stuff, got on our horses, and started up the mountain to the campsite that would be our home for the next week. After we pitched our tents, it started to snow. This was in late May, but snow is not unusual in this area. I realized I was not in Indiana anymore. After getting acclimated to our tents and stowing our gear, we got back on our horses and started looking for the wild mustangs. We didn't see many horses, but the scenery was spectacular. We'd come across a rise and all of a sudden, there would be craggy, impressive, snow-capped mountains right in front of us, so large it seemed you could almost reach out and touch the slopes. And it was like that every day on our rides. Each day, the mountains seemed more majestic. Communing with Mother Nature through the solitude, sky, and land is a spiritual experience. The Sierra Nevada mountains are truly breathtaking.

Our accommodations were sparse. No electricity, no phones.

The only heat was in the big tent where the cooking facilities were. After a day's ride, we would gather back in the big tent where the cook was preparing dinner. At the other end of this tent was a fire pit where we would gather after eating our meals and try to get warm. Since we had no electricity, when it got dark, we went to bed. In the morning, when the sun came up, we got up. I slept in three sleeping bags, two of which were loaned to me by the other riders. Did I mention we had no running water? We had one makeshift outdoor shower. I only took one shower the whole time. It was cold and quick.

At the end of the week, we rode the horses down the mountains to where we had left the cars. By this time, it was hot and dry, and when we reached the cars, I was covered with dust. I said my goodbyes with hugs, jumped in my car, and drove back to Reno to catch the next flight to the Hoosier state. The adventure was not over. I tried to move my next-day flight up to one that night. No go. So I slept in the Reno airport all night. I didn't get much sleep, but I saw a lot of interesting characters. I arrived back in Indiana with a lot of happy memories and new horse-loving friends.

If you ever have a chance to visit that area, please do so. You will be amazed and awed by the beauty of it all. The wild mustangs have to be admired for their spirit to survive independently in the mountainous areas in the West; they are smart, courageous, and elusive. I didn't see as many as I wanted, but maybe next time.

Incidentally, after arriving back home, I received an email from my new horse-loving friends. I was voted Cowgirl of the Week!

Tips:
Some trips are taken with a specific learning experience in mind. Trips with social purposes, such as my trip to help save the mustangs, are part of a larger movement to bring people directly to sites to see environmental problems or endangered wildlife or participate in other worthy causes. Search the Internet for "Volunteer Endangered Species" for links to programs in order to donate your time and energy for wildlife across the world. Some of these experiences are free; many cost money. This book does not endorse any

of these programs specifically. You need to do your own sleuthing and take your own responsibility for setting up your giving activities.

Church and humanitarian groups often make trips to Haiti or to do missionary or economic growth work in Africa. Several groups recruit or accept those wishing to go to clean up water supplies, teach villagers how to start small businesses, build schools or churches, or teach or train teachers. Two respected groups are the African Christian Foundation and the Christian Foundation for Children and Aging. Jewish seniors who wish to serve or financially support groups abroad can contact the American Jewish Joint Distribution Committee, "The Joint," which is active in more than one hundred countries abroad. Specialties such as a background in medicine or engineering are especially welcome. Projects Abroad accepts seniors who want experiences in helping in veterinary medicine, medicine, journalism, sports, education, and other rewarding interests.

Cost Conscious? Educational and social concern trips are available right here in Indiana at our state parks for small fees, given at specified times by park rangers. As one example, Native American interpretation experts offer insights on Indiana's Native American history and culture at Prophetstown State Park near Lafayette. This is the region of Indiana's historic Battle of Tippecanoe. Frequent ecology programs and hikes are available at all of the state parks. You my observe bison at Ouabache State Park and wolves at Wolf Park near Battle Ground. Though the state has no wild mustangs, you can ride horses at Brown County and Fort Harrison state parks, among others.

18

Parachuting–Jumping for Joy

There may be some activities on your to-do list that you think will never happen. They are just impossible, too far out. Upon investigation, you may be surprised at how easy and accessible one of your wished-for activities is. The most far-out activity that I wanted to do, but thought unattainable, was parachuting. Out of the blue, in 2008, I was offered the opportunity to do just that—jump out of an airplane. It all happened because I read an article in the newspaper about an organization named Never Too Late that encouraged and helped older citizens to do something they had always wanted to do in life, but hadn't. The organization is now defunct, but it opened a great door for me while they were functioning.

I dug for the phone number of the organization and explained to the man in charge that I admired his organization for what they offered persons of a certain age. While chatting, he asked my age (seventy-five) and if there was something I had always wanted to do. I quickly replied, "Of course—jump out of an airplane." He said, "You know Sky Dive in Greensburg gave us a gift certificate for a free parachute jump. Would you be interested?" Oh my gosh! Of course I'd be interested—dream fulfilled. I was already jumping for joy!

I drove alone (my grandson was going to go but at the last minute had something more important to do) to Sky Dive. When I arrived, I walked into the small flight building with parachute paraphernalia hanging from the walls and ceilings. I checked in with the man in charge, then sat down and viewed a video explaining the bare essentials of what was going to happen: preflight, flight, post-flight. The restrictions for parachuting are few: weight limit is one, but not age. A ninety-year-old man had jumped previously, and I was informed that provisions are made to accommodate physically handicapped persons. Like many athletic pursuits, you must sign a personal safety waiver. It is always best to contact the individual parachute center for all the rules and regulations.

I was fitted for a harness with straps around my shoulders, waist, and each leg that covered a provided blue jumpsuit. I was then introduced to my tandem partner, Dan, nicknamed "Crash." Hmm... by this time, I was so out of my element, it seemed a bit surreal.

My parachute package included a photographer who would film and photograph me through the whole procedure. Before boarding the small plane on this bright, beautiful day, I was interviewed as to why I had always wanted to do this. I was probably looking and sounding a bit apprehensive at this point. After the interview, Crash and I walked to the plane. My faithful photographer, also a parachutist, continued to film and ask me questions on the plane. He said he would jump out of the plane ahead of me so he could get in a position to film me as I jumped. He told me to smile when I jumped. Really?

The interior of the small bare plane wasn't luxurious, just metal benches along the sides of the plane. The plane was unbelievably noisy, the sound of the motors being amplified as we ascended higher and higher into the atmosphere. Crash, sitting beside me, leaned into my ear and said, "Only one person has chickened out at the last minute." He must have read my mind or observed my ashen complexion. He then said, "It's time to stand up." He hitched himself to one of harnesses on my back to create the tandem—he's the one with the parachute. We walked slowly towards the open door. The three solo jumpers and my photographer jumped out first. I was standing in the open door of an airplane thousands of feet in the air! In my last fleeting moment of sanity, I found beauty in the scene. I could see the curvature of the earth, the pastel outline of the horizon. It was breathtaking.

Here's how it went: "What in the hell am I doing?" Too late! Crash says "Jump!" And we did. The wind crushed my face. Remember that smile I was told to have for the photographer? Forget it! The wind felt like five Gs. My face was so distorted (later seen by many on my provided comedic video) that it doesn't look like me. I have seen pictures of people jumping out of planes, arms stretched out, with smiles on their faces. Those photos must have been photo-shopped. There is no possible way a person could muster a smile when hit in the face with the velocity of hurricane winds.

Crash had told me that we would be free-falling for about fifteen to twenty seconds. Free-falling is just that: falling, falling through the air at a rapid, rapid rate. We were free-falling for what I suspect was not fifteen seconds but fifteen minutes. He finally pulled the cord, and the wonderful white parachute billowed above us. He forewarned me there would be a violent jerk when the chute opens and that I should have my legs out in front and together. He is right: that was quite a jerk, but forget the legs together. Mine were sprawled out like a crazed chicken's.

Corded handles on both sides of the chute are used to control the direction of the thing. Crash encouraged me to take control of the cords. It is exciting to be able to guide yourself through the air, going left or right. Crash took over and started doing movements that seemed like cartwheels in the sky—not really—but my stomach thought that's what we were doing. I was feeling a little urpy but couldn't say too much for fear of throwing up in the sky and showering my tandem partner—probably not a new experience for Crash.

We floated gently towards the earth, and I was instructed to keep my legs straight out in front when we land. We landed softly in the tall green grass. I was still a bit woozy but made a concerted effort to jump to my feet, get untethered from Crash, and unhitch all the harnesses. The other jumpers congratulated me on my first successful jump. I staggered into the flight building, sat down for about twenty minutes, and finally gathered my equilibrium. I later plopped into my earth-bound auto and drove home, adrenaline still keeping me flying high.

George H. W. Bush has said it all: "Just because you are older, doesn't mean you have to sit around and drool. There's lots to be done out there." He was preparing to sky-dive on his eighty-fifth birthday. Would I do it again? You bet!

Tips:

Don't think that something is out of reach. If you do enough research, you may find that your desired activity is not only accessible but close to home.

Take the responsibility disclaimers and personal-safety waivers seriously and realize the risks involved in any of these high-challenge activities. You are opening yourself up to possible injury or worse if something goes wrong, and you need to fact that squarely. On the other hand, the chances of something going wrong are quantifiable, and you should ask how many of the trips up go wrong. That's a disturbing question in this case, but I'd ask it. You will probably find a very, very small percentage. These companies wouldn't be in business if they mismanaged damaging or dangerous experiences.

Cost Conscious? Some sites advertise parachuting in central Indiana for "as low as $129." I give no guarantees on any prices, but if you investigate you can find a reputable program for a fairly reasonable fee as I did. Ask in detail about the safety and performance record of these parachuting companies and read the blogs.

19

Trapezing

While in Florida in December 2010, I had the opportunity to try my hand at trapezing. I have always admired those female trapeze artists on TV. There they are, slim and trim and young, in their sequined bodysuits sailing through the air with the greatest of ease, easily catching the arms of fellow aerialists, making it look so do-able.

I did a lot of hanging upside down when I was a kid, but I didn't know that one day I would finally have the chance to show my trapeze talent. Some goals take a while to fulfill. So, at age seventy-eight, I found myself one night climbing a rickety aluminum ladder to a narrow pedestal board at the top of a circus-type trapeze. The netting below was stretched between the trapeze landings.

The young man in charge had given me a few pointers on the ground. I didn't do too well when he told me to wrap my knees around this little metal bar and fall backwards, then hoist myself upright. The last part was tougher than it had been in my neighbor's backyard some seven decades ago! Soon I was hooked into a harness, climbing the steps to the top to wait for further instructions.

At the top another young man instructed me to hold on to the one stable pole with my left hand and be prepared to quickly wrap my right hand around the trapeze bar that was now swinging my way. He implored, "Now, grip the bar hard!" Incidentally, that bar is very heavy. There's a moment of truth here, as there probably is with all high adventures. It has to do with awareness. I found myself what seemed like the distance of half of a football field off the ground, above the treetops in Florida on a moonlit night, hanging on to that vertical pole with my left hand and anxiously waiting to grab the trapeze bar. The young man said, "When you get a good grip on the bar with your right hand, let go of the pole with left hand, put both hands on the bar, then step off the board, and swing out to the middle." The "step off the board" was the difficult part! My feet failed to move. My newfound instructor/friend, who at this point I wanted to cling to, finally talked (threatened is more like it) me into stepping into the great beyond.

My grandsons on the ground below encouraged me. "Jump, Grandma!" they shouted up. They weren't up here, were they? I did take that step beyond and swung out to the middle of the set with that wonderful safety net below me. I was swinging high above the Florida landscape. If anyone thought I was going to transfer myself to the next trapeze bar that was coming dangerously fast at my face, someone needed to rethink this situation, including those grandsons standing safely on the ground.

I swung back and forth in the air until the law of physics took over and I was hanging dead in the air. Now all I had to do involved another test of faith—letting go and dropping to the safety net below. Finally, I was falling, falling—I hit the net and bounced a bit, but nothing broken. I untangled myself from the net, stood up, and heard my grandsons applauding. Maybe it was worth it after all.

Actually it was an exciting adventure, rather surreal while I was swinging through the air. Had I really gone swinging on a trapeze? Now that I was on the ground, I thought maybe I'd do another swing through the air. Or perhaps not.

Tips:
When you see those lovely, lithe girls who make trapezing look effortless at a circus or on TV, just remember it isn't easy. Give them a big hand and appreciate their talent.

If you are interested in experiencing trapezing as well as some other outdoor challenges close to home, Butler University in Indianapolis offers a Challenge Education program that includes a climbing tower, low ropes course, a trapeze step-off, and more. The free classes start in the summer and are open to everyone over the age of twelve. Most are held in the daytime, but a few are offered at night near the Butler campus.

Cost Conscious? You can vicariously experience circus excitement at the Peru Circus City Festival events in July. At this point, they don't have trapezing experiences for the general public, but you might pick up some tips from the performers. If you live in Miami County, the Circus City Festival will let your children learn to "trapeze." And you can watch these proceedings, too.

Trying the Triathlon

Triathlons have always intrigued me. Swimming, biking, and running. I've done all that since I was a kid. How hard could putting them together be? So at age seventy-eight, I thought why not? It's now or never. I'm not getting any younger. When Ancilla College near my old home in Plymouth announced they would have a triathlon in May 2011, I had the great idea of doing it and dedicating it to Sr. Mary Dolores, my mentor at this same college. She had passed away several years before, but I knew she could be my divine inspiration to get me through this endeavor. She had pushed me to continue my studies, so I knew she would help me now.

I can stay afloat, but realized swimming was not going to be my strong suit. I signed up for swimming lessons at a local spa in January. My female swim coach seemed kind in her assessment of my strokes but did proffer that I had a lot of work to do in the next four months. I certainly admire swimmers. They come to a pool on a midwestern winter day, jump into cold water, swim until they are exhausted, get dressed, and go back out into below-freezing weather.

Bike riding had always come easily, but I thought maybe I'd better get on one before my race. I took off down my driveway, pumped down the hill, and suddenly incurred a wild pain in my knee. I fell off the bike into the grass and practically crawled home. I went to my doctor, who of course sent me on to a knee specialist. He explained my problem in gobbledygook medical terms and insinuated that a seventy-eight-year-old woman had no business in a triathlon. Too bad. I had signed up and paid my entrance fee. I was soldiering on.

Because of my knee, I enlisted my twenty-year-old grandson to do the run, and while signing in on race day, was told he and I could register as a team. He would do the three-mile run, and I would swim five hundred meters and ride my bike for eleven miles.

I was taken to the lake area—yes it was a cold lake in May—and we were instructed to leave the shore in waves. The slower swimmers were to leave last. I slipped into the water and knew immediately this was going to be a long day! The day was beautiful, blue sky above, but the five hundred meters seemed a lot longer in the water than it did on the entrance form. All my well-intentioned swimming instructions seemed to have disappeared. I was now depending on my backstroke with a lot of desperate dog paddling thrown in. At one point, I realized I was the only swimmer still in the water. I looked heavenward and pleaded with Sr. Mary Dolores that if she had any clout up there to please help me get out of this mess!

I finally came close enough to the dock that people were pulling me out of the water. I also realized the people standing on shore were clapping, except my two embarrassed grandsons. When the race was over and we were returning home, grandson John confided that he had to protect my reputation as a triathlete when an onlooker within hearing range jokingly said, "I've seen corpses float faster than she's going." It may be a funny line in some contexts, but not when it is pointed at your grandmother. John strongly suggested that if the man could do better, he should be in the water, not standing on the sidelines making snide remarks, and if he needed any help getting in the water, John could accommodate.

Now all I had to do was get myself out of the borrowed wet suit, get on the bike—the only bike left in the lot—and ride eleven miles on hilly country roads. Needless to say, I was so far behind that the ambulance was following me, and I think he tooted his horn! I finished the bike ride and rode into the area to meet my grandson-John, who was going to do the running. He had given up and gone on before I got back.

It was finally over. The good news (besides surviving)? I received a trophy called the Spirit Award—probably for being the only seventy-eight-year-old woman in history doing her first triathlon.

There were three women on the sidelines watching the award ceremony, two in wheelchairs and one with a walker, who said, "Congratulations! I'm your age, and I couldn't do that."

More good news: Our team came in second. There were only two teams. Would I do it again? Probably not. Would the organizers let me in? Probably not!

Tips :
One thing you can realize if you decide to engage in some of these interesting but super-challenging activities is that you do become a bit of an inspiration to both people your age and those just coming on behind you.

What if you are handicapped, perhaps in a wheelchair? What adventuring opportunities exist for those who aren't running triathlons now? There are many ways to participate in athletic events for those who are in wheelchairs, and these new avenues for adventure increase every day. If you are a handicapped veteran, you can get financial and group support to participate in activities geared especially for you, such as National Rifle Association hunting trips, funded fishing expeditions, and active team sports. Not a veteran? Not a problem. Bowling, billiards, fishing, and team sports such as wheelchair basketball, track, tennis, and even horseback riding are available via organizations listed on the Internet.

But triathlon, yes! The Website for Physically Challenged Triathletes (http:// http://steve_ferang.tripod.com/) gives details about how people of any age can prepare to participate in a triathlon. Of course, you must be in generally good health and have a physical waiver and special assistance to attempt a triathlon, but again the mantra is "Do it! Or at least try it!"

What an age we live in! Bradford Woods, site of Indiana University's outdoor center, sponsors sports activities for the blind. Tennis, golf, racing, and even horseback riding and scuba diving are available for the blind at the Bradford Woods site through a link to the Rehabilitation Hospital of Indiana.

Athletic events are often part of Indiana's many festivals held during the three seasons of good weather. I ran my first mini-marathon at the Plymouth Blueberry Festival years ago. Many towns have their own festivals, and they qualify as adventures, particularly if you eat fried Twinkies or bacon ice cream at one of the many vendors. From the Turkey Trot Festival in Daviess County to the Parke County Covered Bridge Festival, Indiana is a festive state. These events are particularly friendly for seniors.

Related to the festivals are re-enactment events and trail re-creations. The Fulton County Historical Society has reenacted the 1838 Potawatomie Trail of Death (and Courage), westward from near Twin Lakes to the Illinois border and beyond. Markers have been placed at some of the key spots of this tragic event, and at times both Native Americans and history buffs caravan to follow the trip the native peoples were forced to take with federal marshals.

There is a trail along the Ohio River, the Ohio River Scenic Byway, and on further investigation you can come up with walking, biking, and riding trails all over the Hoosier state.

㉑

Tall Ship

One summer I had the opportunity to work on a tall ship for six days. I met my fellow shipmates in San Pedro, California, in June 2004, and boarded the *Exy Johnson*. The *Exy Johnson* is a 111-foot brigantine with two masts, and it had been commissioned the year before my trip. This ship, along with its twin ship *Irving Johnson*, is considered a state-of-the-art twenty-first century vessel. Both are used as teaching ships for "youth of all ages."

Hands-on involvement was encouraged. Every night we had to take down the thirteen sails, roll them up, and carefully stash them in the correct spots. Every morning we unfurled the thirteen sails and put them back up. The *Exy Johnson* had an engine, but our young captain insisted we use only wind power. So after we put up the sails, we still had to wait until enough wind could power us out into the Pacific Ocean off the coast of southern California. (This sailing has to be a male thing; a female would be paddling after about fifteen minutes.)

Once we set sail and were stowing our gear, "All hands on deck" was the cry from up above. We could choose what ship chore we would do for the day, such as cooking, keeping things shipshape (toilets), steering, and standing watch. Another fun thing was standing at the bow watching for buoys, boats, and other hazards. Lots of hands are needed on a ship like this to help with jibing, tacking, and sail handling, and in a stiff breeze we all had to work fast. Some of us attempted to climb the rigging. Your level of participation depends on your ability, willingness to undertake light or heavy work, and personal choice. The literature about this trip said it would be smooth sailing in the waters off the southern California coast. However, seasickness overcame me on the first night. After hanging over the side of the ship for about thirty minutes, I finally gained my sea legs and was able to enjoy the beautiful blue sea and the wonderful food served on the ship. Our chef was loaned to us by one of the culinary schools in the area. Gourmet meals!

In full sail, *Exy Johnson* was beautiful and commanded a lot of attention. It seemed every boater in the water was taking our picture. Our captain commented, "You people are going to be in a lot of photo albums." One day we sailed out to Catalina Island and spent the night in the harbor at Avalon. Sadly, it is where Natalie Woods met her fate. The next day, we left the ship to explore the island.

All of our twelve voyagers, male and female, slept in bunks down below in very small quarters. In the mornings, I had to get up early to use the toilet, the only one in the sleeping area.

Sailing on a tall ship was an interesting experience, and to compare it to kayaking is unfair. I still prefer a kayak where I am in control of movement and I don't have to wait for the wind.

Tips:

Be aware of your own ability to tolerate close quarters. A ship, particularly if it is rolling and unpleasant, can stretch your sociability quotient pretty thin. Nighttime is not the best, as human snoring noises and other exudations can make you wish for your own bed at home.

Actually, this is one trip you may want to take with a friend. I had been invited by a fellow traveler from Illinois whom I had met on a previous kayaking trip in Utah. There was a lot of down time waiting for the wind to pick up, and it was nice to have a friendly ear to bend.

Anti-seasick pills can be helpful. Although the weather was relatively mild, you can encounter rough seas in the Pacific Ocean, especially sailing to Catalina Island. That would be typical in any journey with a tall ship; they do go on the ocean, and the ocean can be rough.

If you are not an experienced sailor, it may be best to try a day sail on a "head boat" before you take the longer overnight cruise. Options for day sails exist in any place where there are tall ships. Day sails generally include lunch, drinks, and beer and are relatively inexpensive for a few hours' experience on the ocean to "test the water," pardon the pun.

Cost Conscious? If you travel to Maine, the home of many tall and other passenger ships, you can expect to pay about $50 a person for four hours on Booth Bay. This is typical of many day sailing ports of call taking sailing passengers.

Gliding

It wasn't enough to jump out of an airplane; I wanted to pilot. My first gliding experience was near Lebanon, Indiana. The small, convenient airport offered gliding sessions on Sunday afternoons. A clear, brisk fall day seemed a perfect time for gliding. I drove to the airport and arranged to go up in a two-seat glider with a trained pilot.

Gliders are attached to the rear of a small airplane with a heavy cord. When the plane takes off and leaves the runway, so does the glider, and you are pulled up into the air. The two-seat glider does not have a motor, so it is very lightweight. In fact, while getting ready to take off, I was able to pull the wide-winged glider into position behind the plane. When the airplane is at the right altitude, the pilot of the plane cuts the glider loose, and the glider pilot takes over, seeking the proper air currents. When you first realize you are actually gliding, it seems euphoric, so quiet. You are just floating through the air. Remember when you made paper airplanes as a kid? Gliding feels as though you are sailing through the air just like your paper airplanes did, though with a lot more control.

The actual pilot of the glider sits in the second seat and does most of the steering. My pilot told me at one point to take over the controls, which was an exhilarating experience. We circled the area a number of times, generally losing altitude as we did, but what a view. We could see the Soldiers and Sailors Monument and the Lucas Oil Stadium in downtown Indianapolis. The pilot took over, and we landed softly on a lovely Sunday afternoon.

Later, I had another glider opportunity in Arizona. My son and I (in separate gliders) glided across the Pleasant Lake area north of Phoenix. It was interesting to contrast the views of the Indiana cornfields with the desert areas of Arizona.

Tips:

Not a good adventure if you are prone to airsickness. Don't eat much before you glide for the first time. It's more enjoyable on an empty stomach.

Be sure you are gliding with a reputable organization. This adventure is not for sissies. Go onto the net and find out what reviews and comments are made there for the particular organization. Google them by name to see if negative postings come up.

Pole Dancing

My adventuring was still in high gear when I saw that pole-dancing lessons were now available in the area. Since I had just celebrated my birthday, I thought this would be a good way to start my seventy-ninth year. I called the owner to inquire about a lesson. When she discovered it was my birthday (and my age), she invited me to take a free lesson. The first class contained four twenty-year olds and me. Our instructor looked as though she had just left a *Playboy* layout. She led us in some exercises that included stretching and writhing on the floor. She strongly encouraged us to lead with our boobs, rear end protruding the other way. We were to transfer all those sensuous moves to one of the eight shiny poles in the middle of the mirror-circled room. She also demonstrated a "sexy walk." This involved throwing your hips from side to side while pointing your toe with each step. I tried to practice this walk at home, and the cat left the room. Actually, pole dancing involves a lot of stretching and is a good way to tone all those unused muscles. It is also great for your posture—in case you want to give it a try.

Tips:

Some adventures may seem to be unsuitable for certain ages, and maybe they are, but that shouldn't stop you from trying them if you want to.

Oregon (2005) on the Rogue River provided many thrills through the rapid rapids. Wilder rapids were awaiting us downstream, with beautiful country and majestic pine trees along the rivers.

Kayaking in the St. Simon's, Georgia, amidst swampy terrain, with wild boars howling in the background.

Climbing on the rigging of the Exy Johnson *to reach the top sail. This ship had 13 sails that had to be cared for twice a day. This was a working cruise so I had the opportunity to work in many areas to get the feel of trying to be a real sailor.*

Exy Johnson *(2004) While sailing in this beautiful schooner in the Pacific Ocean off the coast of southern California, I had the thrill of taking the helm of the ship and barking out orders like our captain.*

Gliding in Arizona: (2005) with my son, Bob. He is being instructed on how to control the glider in the air by a local pilot who sat in the second seat of the glider. We enjoyed gliding over the Arizona desert in the Pleasant Lake area north of Phoenix.

Mustang roundup: (2010) Meeting my equine best friend for a week while observing wild mustangs in the Sierra Nevada Mountains in eastern California. Lite and I had an off-again, on-again relationship while trotting along the mountain trails at 7,000 feet altitude.

Galapagos Islands (2007) The seals on the Galapagos Islands are so friendly and so used to humans you have to rush to beat them to the benches. They love to lounge around with the tourists.

Chloride, AZ (1999) My first kayaking trip introduced me to the old west. Couldn't get any older than Chloride, Arizona which boasts the oldest post office in the state. The jail further down the street didn't look too modern either, and it probably housed some of the old west's bad boys after they got in trouble in Chloride's saloon. The bar is still in business and sports the long wooden bar with the obligatory nude painting hanging over the many-colored whiskey bottles.

Section IV
Adventures of the Mind and Spirit

(24)

Present Tense Only, Please

Why do some people prefer to live in the past tense instead of the present? What's with people saying with a sigh, "Well, in the 1950s it wasn't that way," or "Life was more simple back then"? I once was acquainted with a man who constantly talked about his past. He acted as though he was completely happy in "the good old days." I happen to know that he had a miserable childhood, rejected by his mother, ignored by his father, often disdained by his siblings.

Do people like that dis-remember? Or is it more likely they choose to think that they are not worthy of being happy in the present time or distrust the feeling of being content on the basis that it may be taken from them? Perhaps they feel they don't deserve happiness or contentment in the here and now. It's just easier to say they were happy once in the past. The years gone by cannot be challenged by anyone and cannot be taken from them, so they structure their memories any way they wish.

Contentment is the key word—if one is content, one is happy. And that contentment should not be lodged in the past, a place to which we cannot travel, which we cannot revisit. It is actually all right to admit you are not content in the here and now if it leads to self-assessment, opening a path to better days, a fuller life for what is left of your time on earth. If you feel you are not content in your life right now, remember you are living in the present tense, with an eye to the future. Ask some questions. Do some investigation or self-analysis to find what is missing. What has to happen to bring you contentment? Don't blame someone else in your life—seeking your life's contentment is your job. It's not going to be realistic to say, "Well, I'd be happy and content if only he (or she) would do this or that and be more (whatever)." By this time you should realize that person is not going to change to accommodate you.

I say don't allow someone else to make you happy or unhappy. This whole book has been about charting a course beyond the strictures of life when we are seniors. The whole point is not to let others stand behind us whispering disparaging remarks or to obstruct our way when we chart the course. It isn't easy. Those close to us may stifle us with quiet negativity. If you reveal your desires to someone, and that someone ignores your enthusiasm, it's off-putting. Words I call detour words, such as, "That's a waste of time," or "Do it later," or "Oh, why do you want to do that?" are as discouraging as a derogatory remark. Even our own doubts or self-doubts can get in the way.

Do not depend on others to give you encouragement. For various reasons, others may not want to you to succeed or exceed their lives. That needed push or encouragement must be self-initiated. Resolve to guide your own destiny.

Perhaps it's just that we are afraid of failure. Too many days, weeks, years go by, and we don't accomplish our purpose in life because we are caught in a thought pattern we don't even recognize: what if I fail, look dumb, repeat past patterns of not doing things well, etc. etc. etc. The Failure Club is a Web series dreamed up by Morgan Spurlock, the producer of *Supersize Me*. Spurlock was deeply in debt and had to dig himself out, and his series is about how to move beyond failure. Apparently local chapters of the club are being formed in lots of places to help people make successes out of their past failures. (The Failure Club is probably not a good club to list on your resume, though. "Yeah, I am the president of the local chapter of a Failure Club" may not present you well with an HR person.) The first question a new member is asked is, "What would you do if you weren't afraid of failure?" What would your answer be?

Once we get past the fear of failure, we may fall victim to procrastination. The best sermon I ever heard was given by a man of the flock who said, "The devil always tells us,

'You've got time.'" In other words, we've got time—time to dawdle, time to sit. I am sure he was thinking of spiritual goals, but it works for all goals. As my mother drilled into my head, "If you've got something to do—get it done!" Too many times we have goals, but that first step in the implementation of the goal, is difficult. Often we need a hand from above to get us going, a spiritual nudge perhaps. Speaking as a sometime writer, that blank piece of paper or blank computer screen in front of me can be intimidating. Put one foot (hand) in front of the other to pick up a pen or pencil, or hit the first letter on the keyboard, to get started. What is it about humans that we like to put things off? Maybe fear of failure again.

Habit and society's expectations play a role. For many years I was stuck, as many women are, in a process of making others happy. Maybe I did not want more from life, or at least that is what I told myself. I have decided that persons who have many wants or needs, on the other hand, get more. There comes a time, ladies and gentlemen, when you want to stand up for yourselves—be strong, be assertive, and fulfill a few needs. I don't care if it isn't ladylike or gentlemanly. Get up and go and live!

Tips:

There are specific actions that can move you out of the comfort zone and into seeking new experiences:

Try not to live by a calendar alone. Present tense, please, not past. Consciously avoid living in a state of regret. When you wake up in the morning, determine to make that day a positive one in whatever way you can.

Take one simple step. If you have a computer and access to the Internet, Google what is happening in your town today. Find a festival, a lecture, an art display, a library workshop. Sign up without asking anybody's permission and determine to actually attend. Get the bus schedule, arrange to go with a friend or someone from your living center, or call a cab if your transportation is iffy. If you're not computer literate, get your local newspaper. Don't throw away your neighborhood paper or shopping guide. Good suggestions are often in these local papers, and the events they advertise are nearby.

Check out library notices or bulletin boards at the grocery store. Take classes in writing memoir or a novel, putting out a non-fiction book, collecting your poems, or writing for magazines at the local writers' center. The Writers' Center of Indiana, offering scores of classes year-round, is in Indianapolis and is inexpensive to join. They specialize in "Getting Started with Your Writing." The Kurt Vonnegut Memorial Library also can help you get acquainted with this contemporary and challenging author who grew up in Indianapolis but belongs to the world.

Develop your skill in needlework by taking advanced classes in quilting, embroidery, or knitting. Notices are put up in the shops that sell supplies for these crafts. Develop art skills you have put aside or create new ones by taking classes at an art center. The Indianapolis Art Center in Broad Ripple offers classes in everything from pottery and sculpture to metallurgy, glass artistry, watercolors, and pastels. The Marilyn Glick School at the center has classes for all levels of achievement, from just learning through master classes. Local community colleges offer art and literature and scores of other classes. That's where I got started!

Remember that Indiana has more than sixty-four regional senior citizens' councils, many with centers offering interesting opportunities for growth of all sorts as well as making new acquaintances. How about woodworking, jewelry making, playing the violin, aerobics, dancing, or designing your own Web site? You could even learn to play shuffleboard.

Don't count out developing a laid-aside or new skill in music. It's a real adventure to take up the clarinet again after fifty years have passed since you performed in the IU or Purdue marching band. Look for news of jazz bands, concert bands, and clown and entertainment bands. Some are connected with colleges or universities and actively seek seniors with a good work ethic. New Horizons Band of Indianapolis for seniors is part of the New Horizons International Music Association created by Dr. Roy Ernst. It's a real commitment to join a performance band, but oh, so rewarding. One of these rewards comes for both musicians and audiences when the New Horizons Band plays at central Indiana retirement homes. Ernst believes seniors enjoying music have discovered a "luxury." I say they have discovered adventure!

How about singing? Barbershop, jazz, classical (as in the *Messiah*), all are open to seniors.

An example or two in the state: Tippecanotes Men's Barbershop Chorus practices once a week in Lafayette and welcomes visitors. The Barbershop Harmony Society in Bloomington will let you sit in and/or sing with them at their practice sessions. Ladies, check out the Capital City Chorus, (a chapter of the international Sweet Adelines).

Here's another suggestion: As you reach out for adventure, don't always limit yourself to "oldsters" groups. Adding your talents to a mixed-age group will provide fun and stimulation for both them and you.

Shyness

To step out of the mold and actively seek new experiences requires a certain degree of courage. I was told I was shy when I was a girl, and when you are told that so much at a young age you are what you are told. So I was shy. I do think genetics has something to do with it, although the shy gene has not been definitively identified as yet. My father was quiet, so I guess I inherited my shyness.

Shyness can be debilitating and fills a person with doubt and fear—fear of saying the wrong thing or of being laughed at. Shyness is easily misunderstood. One of my most humiliating moments occurred in eighth grade when I had to give a speech. Not being one of the most popular girls in the class, I knew I wouldn't get much moral support. The desk of the biggest loudmouth in the class was in the front row, and that is where I had to stand. He sneered at me the whole time I was mumbling through my speech. If I looked up at all, it was just to see his off-putting puss. Fellow eighth-graders are probably the most ardent critics that one will meet in life. The pain of that speech haunted me for years. Wouldn't it be gratifying to go back and replay some of those awful moments in your young life with the perspectives we supposedly now have acquired? A movie should be made about that—oh yes, someone did, *Back to the Future*.

I was burdened with shyness until the age of thirty-five when I suddenly thought one day, "I am no longer shy." I'm not sure what happened. I wasn't struck by lightning and didn't experience any near-death drowning (that was before my triathlon) but knew I was no longer shackled by shyness.

How do you get over shyness? Looking back, I would say confront the monster! Learn to speak in front of others. The number-one fear we humans have is of public speaking. Have you ever noticed that schoolteachers don't have this reluctance? They stand before crowds and speak away with wide smiles on their faces as if everybody in the audience is their best friend. Sometimes it's hard to cut them off. Why is that? Because they have spent years before their classes making speeches. They are perennially "on." You can get that type of familiarity and relaxation before crowds too if you make up your mind to do it.

But more than that, if you have been hesitant about getting involved in exciting activities as a senior, it will help you get over that hesitancy about people and substitute confidence for reluctance.

Tips:
Accept an officer's post in a local club or lead the Bible studies class or book club. Being responsible for planning, taking notes, and reporting to the group will give you good experience at being in the public eye, even in a small way.

Join a local chapter of Toastmasters. They specialize not only in speaker training but also in leadership experience.

Take a speech class at the local college or university and get up in front of other people every chance you get. If you can conquer your fear of speaking in front of others comfortably, you are way ahead of your peers as you plan to enjoy this new phase of your life.

If you are required to speak before a group, you may want to consider typing or writing out the entire speech and then practicing it so you can look up, smile, and be comfortable giving it. Speaking from note cards is difficult for some people.

26

Putting Your Own Stamp on Religious Experience: Or Not

Those who have faith traditions often like to expand their participation in church, missionary work, or evangelizing activities in their later years. Church and synagogue volunteers go to prisons for Bible reading sessions. They visit shut-ins and hospital patients. They give out food to the homeless under bridges downtown. These are soul-nurturing activities for both those given gifts and the givers, and they draw attention to the fact that our inner selves need to be cherished. A bit more leisure affords the time for retreats and discovery weekends for Catholics, Protestants, Jews, and Muslims. In addition, you can go beyond into active ministry. Most religious groups allow those who commit to higher studies to take instruction and find some kind of pastoral ordination or lay service on a limited basis. Christian Theological Seminary in Indianapolis offers individuals age sixty-two or older half-price tuition on any of their classes. What a good opportunity.

My own perspective is that living in the later decades allows for individual soul-searching. Sometimes, when I get irritated with my own faith's worship services or the doings of its clergy, I think I'd like to become a Buddhist. I discovered visitors can explore the Buddhist religion and Tibetan culture in Indiana at Dagom Gaden Tensung Ling Monastery near Bloomington. Monks train and observe their religion there, but visitors can sign on for religious, cultural, and educational programs. The so-called "years of wisdom" may be a time to discover how other people worship: There is a Baha'i Center of Worship in Indianapolis, and Orthodox Christian churches, cathedrals such as Sts. Peter and Paul in downtown Indianapolis, and major temples in larger cities allow for tours that provide some information on the faiths.

It can be enlightening and sometimes fun to attend smaller churches out of your faith tradition in a small town you visit with relatives. My own soul searching and temptation to chuck it all at my church and go to the Buddhists comes from a frustration my new independence of spirit has given me with regard to rituals, dogmas, and dogmatic clergymen. As a lifelong Catholic, I love Jesus and my angels. Mary has helped me along the way. But I don't like to sit in church and hear political preaching from the pulpit. I don't want to hear about church and state and religious freedom controversies as part of homilies. I have found that even religious people are preaching political views from their vaulted perches. There have been moments lately when I want to raise my hand, stand up, and say, "Wait a minute. I disagree with that remark." Then I look around at the other pews and parishioners are nodding and agreeing with the minister. Maybe it's just me. I would like to apologize for my independent thinking, but I won't. God gave me an intellect, and I am going to use it. Thank you God!

I think many people are like that and arrive at their own understanding both of and with God. They have either taken God into their lives by this time and made a comfortable, forgiving friend out of Him, a loving father power we want to do nice things for, or they have given up a while ago.

There's probably an understanding about suffering, too, which is a part of most religions. You can believe you have taken your own trip to the Coliseum to face the lions through the sacrifices and disappointments sixty or seventy or eighty years of life have brought you. You relate a little bit to what the ancestors in the faith went through. Spiritual matters mean more to us, but not always in the form of church chicken dinners, observing all holidays by being present in the temple or church, or sewing circle meeting attendance every single week. I recently viewed a TV program about a renowned Jewish scholar who was just issuing a new version of the Talmud. This bearded octogenarian told the interviewer, "God is my friend.

He's everything to me, and I just like to wake up in the morning and say 'Hello, glad you are there.'" And he advised the listeners to devote each day righteously to helping somebody walk his or her own walk as he takes his journey.

That's the kind of God and religious practice I know and appreciate.

Tips:

Understanding your own faith tradition and practice is good, also. It's been many years since catechism or church membership class or bar or bat mitzvah. Most faiths these days have study sessions on the history, culture, traditions, and membership of their religious group.

Try to have some patience with your faith tradition if you feel you've been around too long and know too much. Sometimes the human representatives of the Deity on earth look like bozos. But don't give up. God doesn't change or make mistakes, even if our human institutions do, and you may at some point need the comfort and tradition church association offers. Still, don't be afraid to be an independent thinker. I think God intends for us to be considering, thoughtful worshippers.

The Face-lift

Now let's go in a completely different direction—a little fun.

Working beyond retirement or starting a new business; traveling around the city, state, or world; accepting and trying physical challenge in the out-of-doors and deepening one's spiritual life—of course! Wonderful.

But there are all kinds of ways to expand your spirit, and they don't all happen on trips to far-flung places or trapeze tryout attractions or churches. Trying a daring change to your body may lift your outlook on life. Perhaps it's sensible dieting and working out. What a joy to look at an altered and slightly less bumpy shape in the mirror. Even a little bit helps. In my case, as a skinny Minnie, I decided on a face-lift.

A funny thing happened on my way to the face-lift. As I've frequently said, a woman should experience things in life she can afford and some things she can't afford. A face-lift is the latter, but I succumbed to the thought of a marvelous rejuvenation just at the moment I needed it. I was beginning to feel like Miss Piggy when she exhorted her make-up man, "Just fill in the cracks!" Call it vanity, selfishness, forestalling old age, or just being tired of looking in the mirror and wondering who that old bag is. Isn't it funny how we feel the same on the inside as we did at eighteen, but our outside, we realize, has become part of the wrinkle-city crowd? You know what's worse than a reflection in a mirror? When you are getting in your car and you suddenly catch sight of your face in the back window! Eeeeek! How can I look this old and still be upright?

If you don't feel old, why should you look old? Besides, I am tired of all the store clerks calling me "Hon." I suppose it is short for "Honey" and encompasses everyone with grey hair. What's even worse is when the sixteen-year-old parking attendant asks me if I need a blue handicapped spot, and I haven't even got out of the car yet!

Well, anyway I decided to have a mini-face-lift—the mini was offered at a reduced price. A sale on face-lifts? How sweet!

I visited my local plastic surgeon's office, where previously I'd had a little, just a little, Botox. She said I was a good candidate for a mini-lift and to start eating pineapple because it helps the healing process. She also gave me a form for my family doctor to fill in and to assure her I was healthy enough to go through the procedure.

My family doctor looked askance when I told him why I needed his signature and probably wondered why any seventy-five-year-old woman would even be thinking about a face-lift. Things went well until he checked my heart and detected some kind of irregular rhythmic hiccup. Next I had to make an appointment downtown with a heart specialist and undergo a stress test. Went home and ate more pineapple.

No surgery until I got the results from the heart specialist. This was going to be a few nervous days. On the way home, I stopped at a Dollar General, and while browsing, I spied an ornamental rock that had "Serenity" carved into the top. For some reason, I figured I was supposed to find that rock, a spiritual message. Be serene and things would work out. I bought the rock and went home and ate more pineapple.

I received results: everything OK. I could have the face-lift. It was scheduled for the early part of July. After the surgery, which incidentally hurt, I was sent home to recuperate with lots of pills, instructions, and a paper seven-day post-op diary. The plastic surgeon advised me to write in my diary every day how I felt.

The first post-op day: Numb. I could not sleep with all the bandages. (Note: Do not do this again.)

Second day: Bandages taken off. Lots of swelling.

Third day: Took my first shower to get blood out of my eyes.

Feel better but dizzy.

The next few days contain lots of notes about black-and-blueness.

Post-op day 7: Glad I had this procedure done. Face does look better.

Would I do it again? My motivation was to have the experience of undergoing and recovering from a face-lift operation and understand it as part of my adventure philosophy. Oh, who am I kidding? I did it for vanity's sake. Oprah recently asked Jane Fonda, "What do you see when you look in the mirror?" She quickly replied, "Good work!"

Tips:
Go for it if you can.

I hope you like the taste of pineapples. They must have helped me. I healed in record time.

Don't know about breast lifts. No opinion about those. The experiencing could be uplifting, though.

28

Getting a little Culture On: Shakespeare

My late-blooming college education didn't allow for advanced literary classes. For years I've heard Shakespeare quoted (supposedly the most quoted writer in English) and have had very little idea what those plays were about. I decided to read them, one by one, until I got tired of this adventure.

Here's how that happened. I got my inspiration in the cold of winter. February is a strange, dragging, usually gloomy month. February is also a short month, except in leap years when we get another day of February. Who needs another day in February? Aren't twenty-eight days of boredom enough? In the Midwest, it is the end of winter, which means fluctuating temperatures, between zero and (this year, 2012) sixty degrees, some years major snowstorms, lately spring bulbs coming up and people playing golf. Still, always lots of gray skies. Didn't Shakespeare write *A Winter's Tale*? Maybe I was getting some kind of a message when I thought of that a while ago in the dead of late winter.

To make matters worse, February is an in-between sports month on TV. When I found myself watching a game of rugby, I realized I needed a new challenge. A bunch of men running around bumping into each other with rough behavior as the goal: a poor-man's football. I knew this sport's futility was *Much Ado About Nothing*. It was a time to turn off the TV and add some culture to my life. Expanding my mind and pouring in the words of Shakespeare would be my February goal. Ah ha! Shakespeare here I come.

I started with *Macbeth*, about the Scottish soldier who thought he could outsmart the three sinister sisters—witches who were stirring a pot of newt eyeball stew and mumbling "Double, double, toil and trouble" out in a field. Of course Macbeth's wife didn't add too much to the marital bliss, but she did wash her hands a lot. Things just got darker and danker in the dimly lit castle until they both met their bitter ends. Talk about a downer.

I moved on to *Merchant of Venice*. Shylock was an interesting character who seemed wronged for the wrong reasons. There was a matter of usury. I did like Shakespeare's characterization of the women of the play. Portia and her friend Nerissa outsmarted everyone, including Portia's beau Bassanio, by pretending to be lawyers. I have met some actual pretend lawyers in my own life. If all of Shakespeare's women were like these two strong, competent females, I was becoming a real fan.

It appears there is more than one thing rotten in Denmark besides Hamlet, Danish prince, who is falling off the edge after talking to his father's ghost. Besides Hamlet, his stepfather/uncle is not smelling too good either. Ophelia also proves that too much water is not good for the soul.

I invite you to expand your literary knowledge—pick up a book of Shakespeare. Or do it the easy way, viewing a video with a synopsis propped in your lap. You may discover how easy it is to create a *Comedy of Errors* with your knowledge of Shylock's downfall or the attributes of Portia. Get acquainted with Rosencrantz and Guildenstern. *Measure for Measure*, owning a knowledge of Shakespeare's words should be downright impressive in almost any setting, especially on Jeopardy.

Ah, *All's Well that Ends Well*—I declare February as Shakespeare's month! Join in.

Tips:

There are other good classical writers either in original book form, e-book, or on film (usually on PBS), available at libraries in one form or another. Earn yourself a PhD right on your couch. Here are some good ones:

Pride and Prejudice, Emma, and *Mansfield Park* by Jane Austen
Bleak House, Great Expectations, Little Dorrit, The Mystery of Edwin Drood, and *David Copperfield,* by Charles Dickens
Brideshead Revisited, by Evelyn Waugh.
Also Mark Twain and Jack Kerouac—the long list is available at your library for borrowing or online for purchase.

Your community college or university has classes in the great literature of the world. Try them out! Some can be taken online, but the fun of being in a group for discussion, particularly with attendees the age of your grandchildren, stimulates your thinking. And remember, giving yourself a senior-level education and choosing your own courses is a true adventure in life.

One great way to absorb Shakespeare is to watch video versions with the world's best-recognized actors now on DVD. They may be old, but we have decided, haven't we, that old isn't a bad word. Taylor and Burton's *Taming of the Shrew* is pure pleasure, as is *King Lear* where John Hurt plays the fool—and there are many others.

Cost Conscious?
Ivy Tech Community College throughout the state has been offering courses to seniors free for some years, and literature classes are among the choices. The program is called "Senior Scholars" and is as near as your computer or telephone.

29

Talking to Spiders

You can expand your consciousness by noticing little things, particularly in the animal kingdom. Moments spent valuing the stupendous beauty of the cosmos God has created are part of the meaning of years past the middle of life.

In that large house where my husband and I raised our children, five bedrooms and a three-car garage, was a full basement with a room I called the laundry room. Probably it's more of a multi-purpose room. It contained a washer, dryer, stand-up freezer, sewing machine, and an ironing board. It also was home to many spiders who liked to scurry across the tile floor. Fortunately, I am not a woman afraid of these little critters, running around screaming about spiders. I might scream about other things, but not spiders. One day, I saw a little spider running towards the bottom of the washer. I leaned down and talked to her. She actually stopped and seemed to listen to me, unlike everyone else in my household at the time. She stopped her frantic run—she really stopped! It was then I made the discovery that you can talk to spiders.

I recently reread *Charlotte's Web* by E. B. White. This man had a deep curiosity and an apparent appreciation of the little arachnids. He grew up in a rural home with a big barn that housed not only big animals but small ones, too. Through his observations in the barn, he learned to appreciate spiders enough to write a book about one and create a famous children's character.

I found the book interesting because I too learned to like the little ones, so I am proposing a "Learn to Like Spiders" week. Diane Keaton, in the Woody Allen movie *Annie Hall,* did a disservice to my little friends with her screaming and acting all goofy over a little spider in her bathtub, even if it was "the size of a Buick." Now it is time to honor them.

Let's all try not to be afraid of spiders. Some of this can be done by simple resolution: tell yourself to pause and look a moment before running away or smashing the little critters. Spiders do a lot of good work ridding the world of obnoxious little bugs—bugs you can't communicate with. A spider in my house will always find a safe refuge. Occasionally, a spider will terrify one of my granddaughters, who screams as loud as Ms. Keaton. I return her scream with a scream of my own, "Do not kill that spider!" I will then carefully collect the non-dangerous intruder in a tissue and take her outside so the screaming can stop. I hope she can make a new home outside.

Reasons to appreciate spiders:

No. 1: Their webs are a master of engineering. Two kinds of silk are used to make the webs—moist and dry. Apparently the spider knows when to employ the right web.

No. 2: The spiders' legs have seven joints: roxa, trochanter, femur, patella, tibia, metatarsus, and tarsus. If some of these names sound familiar, it is because some of the names are the same as those of bones in human legs. Another connection we have with the spiders of the world: we're bone related.

One other reason—when no one in your life is listening to you, find a spider. She is a good listener, and no back talk! Seriously, getting in touch with nature is one of the things we can enjoy now that we have more time than we did in the middle years of life.

Tips:

Your local city park system will offer tours that focus on spiders and other insects.

To really appreciate Indiana out-of-doors with all its fauna and flora, you may want to have the adventure of camping. Again, our magnificent state parks and recreation areas give you prime opportunities to be right in nature. Indiana Dunes State Park has three miles of beautiful sandy beaches. Chain-of-Lakes lets you get out on the natural waterways of the state, and at Brookville Lake, you can go up in a seaplane, to cite only a few interesting challenges. In fact, the statistics at Indiana's state parks are impressive: 8,400 campsites, 600 total miles of trails, 75 marinas, 16 swimming pools, and much more. There are activities for the wheelchair-bound at many state parks and recreation areas.

There are also more than one hundred RV parks in Indiana, and probably many more counting small ones around a little lake-ette. These campgrounds weren't there in the 1960s when my husband decided our family should have one of the first small buses sold for "camping," a Cortez, self-contained. "You can cook dinner right in the bus," he said excitedly. As if that was a vacation for me. Our dear bus broke down all the time. And I think that's a still a problem—there's surely a magic switch in the skies that begins to analyze travelers and deliver breakdowns as you take off in your RV or cruising sailboat. Be sure you understand the inner workings of both engines and amenities on your RV before you take off. Still, today they can be pretty swanky, and if you stop at a campsite, it is an outdoor experience. But if you drive one of those $75,000-plus buses to Clifty Falls State Park and park it in the RV parking spaces they have there, don't call it camping.

Electronic Adventuring: The Last Frontier

We are not talking about the *Starship Enterprise*; it's much more obvious than that. Living with computers is a challenge in our lives as seniors. I may be talking to a crowd for whom the horse has already left the barn (some old bromides of wisdom still apply in this new age), but I just want to affirm the need for courage here. You may not be able to muster curiosity. Probably most of my older friends have made their uneasy peace with computers quite a while ago, but it seems as if these consarn machines are always demanding more of us: more updates, more new gadgets, more mice that move and mice that don't, cameras, mikes—to say nothing of what this all leads to, which is "social media." Many a grandpa or grandma has gritted his or her teeth and gone onto Facebook simply to keep up with the grandchildren. Perhaps they regretted it; Facebook supplies more information about the millennial generation than we may want to know.

In the 1950s a TV program touted the March of Progress. I guess it's progress. I learned to type on a manual typewriter when I was in high school with a room full of other females. The course name was changed to keyboarding later when males decided they had better learn to type, too. My teacher instructed us to strike keys firmly and sharply. We practiced and practiced j-u-j, j-u-j over and over and then graduated to a-s-d-f j-k-l-;. That was so ingrained in my cerebellum that I was still striking keys when I went to bed. And still, I see and hear a-s-d-f etc. in my dreams.

My first job as a secretary at Caterpillar introduced me to an electronic typewriter—with all the letters on a round ball. We still used carbon paper and erasers in those days. If a mistake was made on a page, sometimes the whole page had to be retyped. Later, when word processors were introduced, they were marvels. Computers can do so much—everything! In fact, they can do so much that I probably am able to use, or am aware of, only about one-fourth of what is available on my laptop computer. They are like a souped-up auto with all the bells and whistles, only I don't know how to pull the chain or push the button and toot.

We live in an electronically marvelous world. As a kid reading the Dick Tracy comic strip, I was enthralled with the watch on his wrist: he used it as a telephone. Yeah, like that's ever going to happen! Well, it has. I have lived long enough to see and hear most of the human race walking around carrying on a one-sided conversation with a phone small enough to fit into the palm of a hand. It's not on the wrist, but close enough.

Frankly, I don't want to hear other people's inane phone conversations: at the grocery store picking through the broccoli, on the corner waiting for the light to change and slurping a slurpy, or sitting in the airport. Those conversations I love. "Hello, what are you doing? I'm at the airport. I'm waiting for my plane." Duh. Hold the presses.

Why did we have phone booths anyway in the olden golden days? So others wouldn't hear our conversations. You walked into the cramped little upright box, foreign to us these days, closed the accordion door behind you, and dialed the number. Then you have what is known as a private conversation. Today I am privy to details of life-changing events: unfaithful boyfriends, sick pets, visits to doctors for hernias, or tough decisions about shredded wheat or raisin bran cereal. Maybe it's easier to communicate by a phone line than in person. Maybe we have a fear of connectedness—or is it disconnectedness? With all these marvelous electronic devices I still wonder if our communication skills have improved.

I don't want to discourage you from digging ever deeper into the electronic worlds that so dominate our lives. Skyping (not the same as my favorite, skipping), texting, and especially Googling for information are priceless and interesting tools for understanding this complicated age and trying to keep in touch with our kids and in-laws now that the telephone booths have all been sent to Mexico, or somewhere. Wait! I don't want to discourage you. It has been estimated that although 75 percent of persons over age sixty-five have a workable acquaintanceship with computer, that means that 25 percent don't. And the older the age group, the more likely the persons are to be computer illiterate. If that's you, forget what I just said. Go to your local Apple Store and see the millennial generation texting and gaming in high gear—and maybe learn something yourself.

Tips:

You will be surprised to know if you already don't, that the newest smartphones are much easier to use than your old cellphones. It you haven't made the leap, I suggest it; these new pink and white and black babies are intuitive, working as you work, thinking as you do. If you want to add some name to your phone list, there is a plus sign. How refreshing! They are operated by touch; a fingertip on one of several icons sends you to your phone call or list, your e-mail or the Internet, or to tunes to play.

There are classes in getting started on the computer at your local senior center and elsewhere. Those who sell the phones offer free classes in using them. A good introductory article about the terminology and essentials is on Wikipedia at http://en.wikipedia.org/wiki/Computer_literacy.

There isn't much for me to say about e-mail, except that I wonder how and what my grandmother would have e-mailed from North Dakota. Would she put a smiley face by her signature? Or if she texted "Arrved. So this is NorDak." Not enough characters to even touch on the snowstorms and drought years. Yawn. Nobody seems to have saved her letters, which I expect were much more interesting than the electronic versions of today.

Cost Conscious? Your public library has a good array of computers that you may utilize for free! They will also teach you how to "go computer."

The Hypnotist: Off the Beaten Path for Sure

Never one to leave any stone unturned, I have turned over some pretty unusual rocks. I made arrangements to attend a one-night class taught by a hypnotist at a local senior center. The class was held in mid-February, that unfavorite month for me, frigid, icy, snowy, not conducive to going out to a class. I had pre-paid, though, so I was going! I walked in the classroom where three other women were sitting and waiting for our hypnotist to appear. We waited and waited. Finally a person from the center came in the room and announced our hypnotist would be there soon. Seems his car battery died—it was that cold!

And he did appear—rather he bounced into the room. Tim was very congenial and affable, and we quickly forgave him for his tardiness. Having recently moved to the area, he was introducing hypnotism to Indy. He explained that he came to realize in a personal way that hypnotism can be helpful. His father had suffered through a recent fire in which he was badly burned. One of Tim's professors in college was a hypnotist and suggested Tim learn the science to help his father get through the pain. Tim's hypnotism helped alleviate the horrendous pain his father was enduring as his burns healed. From this personal incident, Tim knew he could help others and so became a certified hypnotist.

He chose one lady in our small class of four women and asked her to come forward and sit in a comfortable chair. She told us all that she was living with a lot of physical pain and some unspecified personal problems. Tim talked softly and told her to close her eyes, as he continued to talk to her alone about her pains and how those had affected her. He asked her to gather all of her pains/problems and put them in a basket, then encouraged her to envision walking through a lovely, sun-filled meadow. She was to think of her pains as small stones, and as she walked slowly through the leafy meadow, she would drop the stones, ridding her physical being of the pain. The session lasted just a few minutes, and when the hypnotist told her to awaken, she opened her eyes and smiled. I asked her later in the class how she felt, and she said she did feel relieved and she believed the session would help her cope with her problems.

He asked all of us why we were there and what we expected from his class. I was the last to respond. When he heard about my travels and adventures, he convinced me that I should share my story with other women. He was the first person to push me to get going, give speeches, and motivate other people and eventually write a book. Tim is truly an inspirational person. He has helped many people through hypnotism to stop smoking, lose weight, and enjoy a better life. Tim is on the way to gaining national recognition, and from what I could observe, he deserves it. Since meeting Tim, I have seen several hypnotists on TV, and they are being met with increasing acceptance, at least for some people.

A hypnotist may not be your cup of tea, but don't disregard something/someone with preconceived ideas of what you have been told. No hocus pocus in what I saw!

I have also visited a psychic in Indianapolis. No hocus pocus here, either. And no, she did not gaze into a crystal ball. She is well known in her field and has worked with the Indianapolis police force as well as individual clients across the country.

My daughter first visited her and was amazed how much knowledge she had not only about her but of the whole family. My curiosity was tweaked enough that I made an appointment with her, too. I learned that a good psychic does not tell you what to do and when to do it. What she does do is to explain what you could accomplish and then expects you to chart the course to meet that end.

This is just another avenue you may explore if you get your "daring" shirt on.

Tips:
Get the most from exploring for adventure by utilizing the three Cs of curiosity, courage, and challenge on the "outer limits."

You may also want to tell yourself not to take life so seriously. There's a spirit of fun and almost childish expectation in seeking new adventures, particularly unusual ones. It's called open-mindedness, and we all may be surprised what we find once the door to new experiences is opened. It can become a habit and it helps ward off the three Ds: depression, dependency, and dopiness (make out of that what you will).

Hypnotists are listed on the Internet and in phone books and offer the power of their suggestion to quit smoking, alleviate pain as Tim did for his father, improve confidence, and uncover hidden problems.

If you do have an interest in psychics, you may want to read Sylvia Browne's books. She has been both praised and debunked for successes and failures at seeing beyond the veil. Sylvia recently appeared at Lucas Oil Stadium and may be in our area again to lecture. Hearing a psychic speak, you may decide for yourself whether it has anything to it.

(32)

The Ultimate Adventure: Writing a Book

How many friends or acquaintances have you heard say, "I should write a book"? Whether that person is being facetious or realistic, it's a common desire: the idea has crossed just about everyone's mind.

I had thought about it for years, and after some research and investigating, I found the editor/publisher of this book, who encouraged me to get my thoughts in some kind of book order and provided support on how to do so. I had been thinking of writing a book for years. I wrote it on every to-do list for at least fifteen years, and maybe longer. I even wrote it on grocery lists: bananas, milk, bread, write a book. I sat in church and prayed for a nudge from above, "Help me write a book." I finally shortened it to just "book." I figured Jesus heard it so often He knew what I was talking about. And finally it happened. That is not a coincidence.

Yours may be a novel-writing experience, or you may have always wanted to write a book about the Civil War or bird watching. I strongly recommend memoir writing. That is the easiest and most accessible type of writing you can do, and if it works for you, it can get you started on other types of writing. Memoir is a tremendous vehicle for another reason: it's important for you to put your life in context, especially after a certain age. I worked in a nursing home in the 1970s and had the privilege of interviewing many of the clients, and I was completely blown away when I heard some of their life stories. One woman had shaken hands with President Grant when he was in the White House. Another woman was acquainted with the original Charles R. Walgreen of drug fame. One woman was born in Appomattox, Virginia, not too many years after the Civil War treaty was signed. My grandson's other grandmother lived in Austria when Hitler took over and assumed power. Her husband was imprisoned by the Nazis, and she had to convince his jailers he was not a dangerous person. When telling her story, she remarked, "I met the one nice Nazi in Germany." He instructed her to take her husband and quickly get out of the country. She helped her family flee the country through some perilous circumstances and immigrate to the U.S. Such a heroine!

Our lives may not have crossed paths with so many illustrious persons in history, but we still have a lot to write about. We have lived through many changes in the world, at least four wars, several revolutions (industrial, technological and sexual), lived through the hula hoop and colored toilet paper fads and safely leaped from one century into the next. Remember the big brouhaha about entering the twenty-first century? All past history now.

If you don't write a memoir for your own satisfaction or to put perspective on your life experience, which you really should do, think about the future genealogists in your family tree. You are doing your future family history buffs a favor by writing down your life story—complete with secrets or thoughts of your growing up and maturing. Put some background of the times, too, including your own loved causes, opinions, political affiliations, and religious perspective and observations on the passing scene. We all live in interesting ages, not unlike the women I interviewed in the nursing home.

I have discovered that writing a book or putting your thoughts in order requires a lot of perspicacity, perseverance, and just plain doggedness. I have talked about journaling when one travels, but writing is stimulated and improved by jotting down descriptions, insights, and impressions of the day. Computers make it easier to journal. Every morning, sit down and just type your thoughts. Never mind the punctuation and grammar; just get words on paper.

It may not end up in a hardcover or softcover book. It can be compiled in a variety of ways these days, and it is the most important book your children may ever read: the story of your life, a major branch in their heredity tree. Your friends will benefit from it too. Assessing what is important to put into your memoir and selecting events and impressions, you may be surprised at how much you have contributed to the world around you. Thus the process itself will help you gain deeper perspectives about the meaning of your life—or maybe even life itself! What you have lived needs to be told. Carpe Diem! Seize the day!

Tips:

I recommend taking a class in memoir writing at the senior citizens center, local college, or social service agency. Flanner House in Indianapolis has classes on memoir writing, as does the Writers' Center in Broad Ripple. Your local town library can steer you towards a writing course, possibly right at that very library. The Knox County Public Library in Vincennes is only one of the very good libraries in our state that offers writing courses.

Books can easily be produced digitally these days in press runs from one to five hundred. The costs for simple paperbacks without frills can be surprisingly inexpensive. You can search "Self Publishing" on the Internet to see what kinds of opportunities are available for your book to be published—that is, if you don't get picked up by a New York agent representing a big publishing house. To find out about agented book contracts, check out Jeff Herman's *Guide to Book Publishers, Editors and Literary Agents, 2012 edition*. But if you decide to self publish, heed my warning: there are many scams and schemes out there to rob you of your money, so read the blogs, investigate carefully, and ask advice of those who have gone the self-publishing route.

You don't have to write a book; you can begin a late-flowering writing career by writing articles for your church newsletter, shopping guide, retirement community newsletter, or one of the magazines or papers in your home county. They are looking for material, so here, as always, take courage, make contact calls, and get busy.

Cost Conscious? Even though most of these courses are either inexpensive or free, you can cut costs even further by educating yourself at the library with copies of *Writer's Digest* or *The Writers Magazine* or consulting books in the research section on learning to write effectively.

As you head out the door to the Shakespeare lecture or the forbidden ski slopes or even to the town not too far from you for that best cheeseburger and visit to the town museum, be aware of these last tips:

Just because you CAN, doesn't mean you necessarily SHOULD.

But on the other hand, if you think you shouldn't try because the new experience is too hard, too strange, or beyond your ability or budget, think again!

If your kids don't call as often as you wish they would, if parts of your body seem to be on slow speed or "off," if the day looks pretty boring and even lonely, remember this:

You have yourself for a companion, and

ALL THE ADVENTURE IN THE WORLD IS WAITING FOR YOU!

You will think of adventures beyond what are in this book. I have only touched the surface of incredible things for seniors to do in our state. If you do exciting things or challenges new to you that you want to share, contact me by e-mail at mariealbertson@att.net.

(2011) We waited in line a long time to see this famous landmark, the Eiffel Tower, twinkling at night.

(2007) Colorful kayaks bob in the water in front of our lodge in Sitka, Alaska, inviting us to get back in the water to explore more of the areas in Sitka Sound. We took advantage of the unusual warm weather to paddle the smooth waters in a golden afternoon. The family of eagles who lived in the nearby pine trees soared overhead.

Colorado River: (1999) my first kayaking trip began on the Colorado River in southern Nevada. We put the kayaks in the river right below the Hoover Dam. I didn't know yet what beauty would enfold me as we paddled around the bend in the river. The feeling of tranquility and the transcendental experiences of the river would last a lifetime.

Morocco (2008) Trying to get comfortable on my first camel ride in the Sahara Desert in Morocco. Camels are marvelously built for the desert but do not provide a pleasurable seat. They also like to spit a lot and most need a date with the dentist.

Morocco: This is a new-found friend: a water man of the Sahara Desert. With all of his bells, whistles and noise makers he was a welcome sound and sight for desert travelers always desirous of more water.

China (2006) wow! My first steps on the Great Wall in China. A life-long dream comes true. The Great Wall was showing her age but is still a marvel to all the tourists, young and old, who visit China to step on her ancient stones.

China (2006) All kinds of tourists and local visitors enjoying a Sunday afternoon walk on the Great Wall. Surprising how many Chinese tourists are on the wall taking advantage of their new economy and the new openness of the country.

Egypt (2020) Visiting the Edfu Temple near Luxor along the Nile river. The statue of Horos, son of Isis and Osiris has the head of a hawk; his crown is made of two parts. The white part represents Upper Egypt (in the south) and the red part represents Lower Egypt (in the north).

Australia (2009) looking apprehensive and pretending to be Indiana Jones, my first attempt at tree surfing (zip lining) in Australia. Climbing through the tropical rain forest at Cape Tribulation in Australia was the means of getting to the top platform where two young Aussies were dishing out instructions and lots of humor. Standing above the trees provided me with a spectacular view of the Coral Sea where the first naval battle of World War II took place.